What parents say about *Calmer, Easier, Happier Screen Time*:

'We'd been having rows about the computer for months so I was really surprised how quickly Noël's method worked with our three children. On the first day of the new screen time rules the two youngest screamed like banshees, but by the end of the week they were accepting the rules, and even smiling when we praised them about it.'

'I was worried that it would be cruel and unfair to limit my children's screen time because most of their friends seem to be on the computer all hours. But I decided I had to be true to my values. And they didn't protest much. Now I'm happier, and so are they.'

'I thought my teenage boys would just laugh in my face when we tried these new strategies. They did laugh at first, but we didn't give up. Now they love the Special Time and Family Time and Descriptive Praise. And they're proud of themselves for being so sensible about their screen use.'

'Homework was a nightmare, trying to police the screens, endlessly chivvying them to stay focused. We decided to put limits and rewards on the screen time, and we also used Noël's homework strategies. Two of our children improved hugely in the first month; the oldest took longer. But we didn't give up. And now homework is peaceful – and even enjoyable!'

'I hadn't realised that too much screen time was making so many other problems: being hyper at bedtime, being grumpy with his siblings, complaining about homework and reading, being disrespectful, not wanting to play outside. I love it that getting back in charge of the electronics solved so many other problems at the same time.'

Calmer, Easier, Happier
Screen Time

ABOUT THE AUTHOR

Noël Janis-Norton is a learning and behaviour specialist with over forty-five years' experience in Britain and the United States as a head teacher, special needs advisor, consultant, lecturer, parenting coach, speaker and author. She is internationally known for her distinctive *Calmer, Easier, Happier Parenting and Teaching* methods, which show parents how to improve family life and which guide teachers to bring out the best in their pupils.

Calmer, Easier, Happier Parenting was published in the UK by Hodder & Stoughton in 2012 and was an instant bestseller on Amazon UK. It is published in the US by Penguin, and it has been translated into French, Russian, Chinese and Italian.

Calmer, Easier, Happier Homework was published by Hodder & Stoughton in 2013. This book teaches parents how to help children do their best at school and with homework – and to enjoy the process.

Calmer, Easier, Happier Boys was published by Hodder & Stoughton in 2015 and was also an Amazon UK bestseller. In this book Noël explains simple, effective strategies for addressing the unique challenges of raising motivated, cooperative and confident boys.

For many years Noël has been fascinated by how to help children learn to do their best and be their best. *Calmer, Easier, Happier Parenting and Teaching* resources are a refreshing mixture of common sense about children and teens, extensive knowledge of child development and expertise in specific difficulties with learning and behaviour.

Through her books and CDs, and through her seminars, courses and talks for parents and teachers, she has helped transform the lives of tens of thousands of families. As Director of the Calmer, Easier, Happier Parenting Centre in London, she continues to work with families and to train teachers and parenting professionals in her highly effective methods.

Noël is a regular speaker at conferences and has been featured on television and radio programmes and in numerous newspaper and magazine articles. She was the 2011 spokesperson for National Family Week, and she is an online parenting advisor for the charity Scope. She is also the parenting expert for Macaroni Kid (a popular website for parents in the US).

Noël has two grown children and six grandchildren.

Calmer, Easier, Happier Screen Time

*For parents of toddlers to teens:
A guide to getting back in
charge of technology*

NOËL JANIS-NORTON

First published in Great Britain in 2016 by Yellow Kite
An imprint of Hodder & Stoughton
An Hachette UK company

1

Copyright © Noël Janis-Norton 2016

The right of Noël Janis-Norton to be identified as the
Author of the Work has been asserted by her in accordance
with the Copyright, Designs and Patents Act 1988.

A CIP catalogue record for this title is available from the British Library

Trade Paperback ISBN 978 1 473 62275 3
eBook ISBN 978 1 473 62277 7

Typeset in Fresco by Hewer Text UK Ltd, Edinburgh
Printed and bound by Clays Ltd, St Ives plc

Hodder & Stoughton policy is to use papers that are natural, renewable
and recyclable products and made from wood grown in sustainable
forests. The logging and manufacturing processes are expected to
conform to the environmental regulations of the country of origin.

Hodder & Stoughton Ltd
Carmelite House
50 Victoria Embankment
London EC4Y 0DZ

www.hodder.co.uk

This book is dedicated to all parents who want to get back in charge of screen time in their homes in order to create a calmer, easier, happier family life.

CONTENTS

Section Three: The Calmer, Easier, Happier Parenting strategies that will make the new screen habits easier to establish

ACKNOWLEDGEMENTS

Once again, when it came time to give thanks to all the special people who have helped bring this book to life, I realised that I've already said it all in my earlier books. It's all still true, so here I will say it again.

My deepest gratitude goes to:

Jill Janis, my sister, friend and colleague, for her wisdom and clear thinking, her valuable advice, her thoroughness and tireless attention to detail, her love of language, her artist's soul, her compassion and her sense of humour when I need it the most! Jill's profound understanding of family relationships has helped me, over the past forty-five years, to hone the principles of *Calmer, Easier, Happier Parenting and Teaching*. Without her, this book would not exist.

Gillian Edwards, to whom I owe a great debt for the extraordinary generosity, understanding and kindness she has showered on me over the last twenty-five years, and especially for holding my hand on the emotional journey of the past year, helping guide this book to fruition. As well as being my PA, Gillian has been my all-hours typist, my problem-solver, my exactly-the-right-word finder, cook, nursemaid and voice of reason – above and beyond the call of duty.

Laura Runnels Fleming, my dear friend and trusted coach, whose focus and dedication are inspirational.

My colleagues, past and present, at the Calmer, Easier, Happier Parenting Centre (in the UK and the US), for their insight, sensitivity and determination, and for sharing my vision of what family life can be:

Heleni Achilleos, Rosalie Ajzensztejn, Nancy Albanese, Isabel Berenzweig, Suzanne Burdon, Miriam Chachamu, Amanda Deverich, Gillian Edwards, Suzanne Ferera, Sherry Fink, Laura Fleming, Lou Fleming, Michael Foulkes, Tina Grammaticas, Ellen Hatvany, Bebe Jacobs, Chloe Janis, Jill Janis, Sara Laksimi, Annie Saunders, Luke Scott, Alison Seddon, Robin Shaw, Grazyna Somerville, Robyn Spencer, George Stergiou, Dorian Yeo and the many others who have also contributed to this work, too numerous to mention.

Nicky Ross, my patient, persistent and understanding editor at Hodder & Stoughton; it is due to her foresight that the 'Calmer, Easier, Happier' series of books is now a reality.

Clare Hulton, my agent, for believing in me, in this approach and in my books.

My children, for the constancy of their support and encouragement.

And finally, my special thanks to the tens of thousands of parents and professionals with whom I have had the privilege of working in the Calmer, Easier, Happier Parenting and Teaching programmes. They have tried this new approach and reported back 'It works!' Their courage and honesty continue to touch and inspire me. I am grateful to them for sharing their stories and experiences for this book and for their passionate support of 'Calmer, Easier, Happier Parenting'.

INTRODUCTION

As I travel around the UK and the US leading workshops and coaching parents, I hear the same complaints over and over again:

'My daughter spends most of her time in her room, and she's on her computer for hours every day. I have no idea what she's up to. When I try to go and see her to ask how her day was, she snarls at me to leave her alone.'

'My teenagers bring their phones to the dinner table, no matter how many times I remind them. We can't even have a proper conversation because they're always texting their friends or showing each other funny videos.'

'Getting my kids off their tablets is so stressful. The arguments! That's why I sometimes pretend I've forgotten about the time and let them have more. But then they don't take me seriously.'

'My kids have got into the habit of watching a programme while they're eating. I can't talk to them about anything because they won't listen.'

'My boy picks up my phone whenever I leave it on the table, even though I keep telling him not to.'

'Screen time is the first thing my kids want to do as soon as they come in the house.'

'There's so much arguing and negotiating about when they can be on their screens and for how long. I can't stand listening to myself – nag, nag, nag.'

'My kids have become devious, just to get a bit more screen time.'

'My son kicked me when I insisted it was time to switch off and get ready for bed.'

I've written this book at the urging of parents who were feeling frustrated, confused and worried. They knew they should be doing something about the problem of electronics in their family, but they weren't sure what to do or how. Throughout this book you'll find simple and effective strategies that will transform your children's and teens' screen habits, resulting in greater cooperation and respect, more mature common sense and stronger self-esteem. You'll all enjoy family time more, and family life will become calmer, easier and happier.

If you're sceptical about these claims because it feels like you've already tried everything, without much lasting success, that's understandable. But you probably haven't tried these strategies yet. It's fine to feel sceptical or suspicious; you don't have to believe that these new strategies will work in order for them to work. All you need to do is keep practising, and you will see the results for yourself.

This is the fourth book in the 'Calmer, Easier, Happier' series. It's a companion volume to the first three: *Calmer, Easier, Happier Parenting; Calmer, Easier, Happier Homework* and *Calmer, Easier, Happier Boys*. Please dip into these books whenever you want more background information about typical parenting issues or more examples of how to put the new strategies into practice.

WHY PARENTS NEED TO GET BACK IN CHARGE

CHAPTER 1
GETTING BACK IN CHARGE

Why are you reading this book? I'm guessing that it wasn't idle curiosity that prompted you to choose this book. Even if you've never heard of me or haven't read any of my other books, you were probably drawn to the title or subtitle of this book. Most likely there are some screen time issues in your home that you're not completely happy about.

Do you want to get back in charge of your children's or teens' screen use? And do you feel you could use some advice about how to achieve this goal? Maybe you're looking for confirmation that you do have a right to get back in charge of the electronics in your home? I wrote this book to share with parents a set of useful tools for getting back in charge, so that family life can be calmer, easier and happier.

It's common nowadays to talk about screen dependency and even screen addiction. When we talk about addiction in relation to screens, we're using that term in a metaphorical sense, but I believe that we need to treat our children's screen preoccupation as seriously as if it were a real addiction. We know that when people are addicted to a substance or to an activity, they will find a way to satisfy their craving even if it is at great personal cost. Parents I've talked to have seen that screen dependency has a negative effect on many important aspects of family life, such as homework and revision, music practice, mealtimes, household chores, bedtimes, getting up in the morning, peer relationships, even tone of voice, respect and family relationships. So there are a lot of good reasons to get back in charge of the screens in your home.

In my work as a learning and behaviour specialist and the Director of the Calmer, Easier, Happier Parenting Centre, I hear from more than a thousand parents every year. I listen to their concerns, and I give advice that will help improve the family issues they are worried about. When I ask parents what their goals are for their children in terms of screens, again and again parents tell me the same thing. They want their children to:

- Learn to enjoy technology wisely
- Develop sensible tech-management habits
- Monitor their own screen use
- Limit themselves
- Prioritise the important things – sleep, homework and revision, spending time with family and friends – before electronics

These are all medium-term or long-term goals. In the short term, parents have an additional goal. They want to protect their children from the harmful effects of the negative values that are so prevalent on screens. Parents recognise that the emotional immaturity of children and teens makes them very easily influenced. Parents want to build a firm foundation of positive values to give children a better chance as they grow up of learning how to protect themselves.

You can draw an analogy with how we feed our families. When our children are young, we make a point of giving them healthy food and guiding them into sensible eating habits. We do this to give them a solid foundation because we know that as they get older, they will encounter many junk food temptations outside of the home. Even if you wanted to shield your children from all junk food, it wouldn't be possible. And even if you could manage it, you wouldn't be giving them the opportunity, as they grow emotionally stronger, to practise making sensible food choices. Similarly, past the first few years of a child's life, it's not possible to keep children in a tech-free bubble, even if you wanted to. The best way to protect them from negative influences is by strengthening their value system.

The underlying premise of this book is that children and teens are experts at knowing what they want, but parents know what is good for their family. Your goals for your children are probably similar to those listed above; in short, you want to guide them to use technology sensibly, and you want to protect them while you can. And if you are like most of the parents I talk to, you want to be able to relax! You want to feel more at peace; you want to feel satisfied that the screen habits your family are developing are habits that are good for them.

But you may not be sure how to achieve your goals for your family. That is what this book is all about. You <u>will</u> be able to achieve these goals. I'm not promising that getting there will be a piece of cake. But the journey will definitely feel calmer, easier and happier than if you allow confusion or resignation to keep you from taking decisive action.

There are several ways parents can respond to the problems of screen dependency. Does one of the profiles below describe the stage you and your family are currently at?

- Have you let the screen situation in your home drift because you haven't known how to tackle the problem? By now you're starting to feel really fed up. You're just about ready to do something decisive, rather than continue to complain, nag or threaten. But you still don't know how to take effective action.
- Maybe you've tried laying down the law, but it seems to have backfired, leaving everyone feeling resentful. You

might be feeling discouraged and powerless, but you
don't want to give up. You want to find a better way to get
back in charge of the electronics in your children's lives.

- Perhaps you've tried to convince yourself that your children or teens are mature enough and sensible enough to
monitor their screen use and to limit themselves when
they can see they're overdoing it. But it's become clear
to you that this just isn't happening. That's not surprising, really. Screen use is so mesmerising and so addictive; it feels so good. That feeling easily overrides your
child's common sense.

- Perhaps you've heard so many other parents joking
about their children's screen issues that after a while
the problems start to feel normal and inevitable. It
seems as if maybe you should just accept the status quo
without feeling upset about it.

Regardless of which stage you're currently at, the positive,
firm and consistent strategies in this book will help you to get
back in charge. You will soon see that electronics can add
enjoyment to family life, rather than adding conflict.

If you feel like blaming your children or teens for their fixation on screens, just think of the times when you, as a sensible
adult, have stayed up too late, against your better judgement,
watching something unmemorable on television. Or the times
you've been lured into checking out just one more Facebook
post or YouTube video. If we, the mature adults that we are,
find it so easy to get sucked into Screen World, just imagine
how much more tempting it is for our children and teens.

It's only when we are in charge, when we are the deciders of
what happens in our homes, that we are able to do our job of
transmitting the values, skills and habits that we believe are
important. When we are not in charge, our children's

immature values will prevail and will be reinforced. I'm sure you've read or heard the advice about making parenting less stressful by 'picking your battles'. What this usually boils down to is avoiding situations that would result in your child or teen whingeing, complaining, arguing, pleading, crying, slamming doors or throwing himself on the floor. The problem with picking our battles is that it's the opposite of the teaching and training we need to do in order to transmit our values, skills and habits. In this context, what I mean by teaching is making sure our children and teens <u>know</u> what they should do. And by training I mean guiding them into the <u>habit</u> of doing what they know they should do.

Children often resist this teaching and training at first because changing habits is rarely easy. It's natural for children to react to new routines and habits and rules with some complaining, crying, arguing or even tantrums – at first. So let's not view this annoying behaviour as a 'battle' to be avoided. Let's think of these negative reactions as immature ways of expressing uncomfortable emotions. A tantrumming child hasn't yet learned how to express his upset in words, or perhaps he is so overwhelmed by the strength of his emotion that he temporarily forgets how to control his actions. Or it could be that this sort of misbehaviour has worked in the past, at least some of the time, to get your child some of what he wants. Whingeing or shouting or arguing might have bought him a bit more time to do what he wants. Or he might have noticed that sometimes you give up out of frustration or exasperation. Or maybe he's learned that the crying and whingeing are guaranteed to get your attention.

Our job is not to avoid our children's negative reactions, but to teach and train more sensible reactions. We will enjoy our role as teachers and trainers much more when we remember that children are, by definition, immature. They want what they want. They believe they need what they want. Let's allow them to feel their childish feelings. Let's not think of their upset feelings or the resulting misbehaviour as a battle. In a battle someone wins and someone else loses. But teaching and training isn't about winning and losing; it's about changing habits.

Being in charge is not a static state of affairs. Over time you will probably refine your values. And as your children grow and develop, their needs will change. You will naturally continue to cycle back through the steps I introduce below until your children leave home.

How to get back in charge and stay in charge

Step One: <u>Assessing</u>

Before you can decide to take action consistent with your values about screen time, you need to discover exactly what's happening. Ask yourself questions about the four screen issues in Chapter 2. Assessing (and reassessing) the current situation includes deciding whether what is happening in your home fits with your values. This step also includes listening to your children's opinions and wishes. However, you will always have the final say because you are wiser and because it is your job to guide children towards the values you believe are right.

Step Two: <u>Planning</u>

In order to plan effectively, first you need to clarify (with your partner if you have one) what your values are. This enables you to decide which rules and routines will guide your children towards those values. It may not be easy to come to an agree-ment with your partner. Although your fundamental values may be the same, how you each tend to put them into practice might be very different.

Consistency between parents can be difficult to achieve. But we don't have the luxury of deciding to 'agree to disagree'. It's not fair to our children to expect them to feel comfortable with two different sets of rules in the same home. In Chapter 8 I explain how a couple can rise above their differences and learn to compromise, to become a United Front, in order to come up with a coherent plan that both are willing to stick to.

To help you prioritise and plan, it helps to ask yourself some searching questions:

- What makes me uncomfortable about the current screen time habits and arrangements?
- Which parts of the day do I feel comfortable about because I can see that my children are developing sensible habits?
- What do I wish was different at home?

When you're answering these questions, don't minimise the problem areas. Don't try to convince yourself that *'This is just how kids are nowadays,'* and *'There isn't much anyone can do about it so I might as well save myself a lot of stress by just accept-ing it.'* If the current situation doesn't fit with your values, you won't be able to accept it for very long. And if you don't invest the time in planning, you're likely to get stuck in a vicious circle of trying to be patient and accepting, then nagging or exploding, then feeling guilty and going back to trying to be patient and accepting.

Here's a good question to ask yourself:

- What do I want a typical week to look like for my children?

It's useful to think of your children's screen activities in terms of a whole week because weekday and weekend routines will be different. Take the time to visualise an ideal week during term time and an ideal week during the holidays. Then stretch yourself to visualise further:

- What do I want my children's typical week to look like next year? In five years? In ten years?

What we focus on and insist on now will shape their habits and their values in the days and weeks and years to come.

There is no one-size-fits-all solution to screen time headaches. Throughout this book I will give you examples of strategies that real families have put into practice successfully. By 'successfully', I mean with rapidly diminishing complaining and resistance, and with children and teens learning (over time, not overnight) to monitor and limit their own screen use more and more sensibly. You can adapt these examples to fit your situation, your values, the ages and temperament of your children, your children's peer groups and your budget.

Step Three: <u>Doing</u>

Step Three is about putting your plans into action: introducing the new rules and routines, following through consistently and insisting, using the most effective and least resentment-inducing methods.

Step Three is also about learning and using the core Calmer, Easier, Happier Parenting strategies. These will help to reduce resistance and improve cooperation, motivation and self-reliance. You will find yourself turning to these strategies many times a day, whenever you want to influence your children to develop more sensible habits.

This step has two parts. The first part is telling your children what the new plan will be. The second part is following through to embed the new rules and routines.

Some of the ways that parents explain and introduce new rules are friendlier and clearer, and therefore more effective, than other ways. In Section Two, I explain how you can introduce your new plan in a way that is likely to get the best possible results. You might not feel that you need step-by-step instructions for this, especially if your children are very easy-going or very young and not yet in the thrall of Screen World. But if your child is quite sensitive or inflexible, or if he is given to big reactions, it pays to prepare carefully. This will help you to avoid most (but not all) of the complaining, arguing and tantrums.

As you put your plan into practice, you will find yourself revisiting Step One many times, assessing the current situation in your home to see the results of your actions. It's tempting to jump the gun, but don't assume a strategy is not working based on how the first week or two go. Stick with a new strategy for at least a month. This gives your child time to get used to the new rules and routines. If a rule or routine isn't going according to plan after a month or so, you will need to pause to assess what went wrong (Step One) and then decide what you want to tweak (Step Two).

Getting in charge of the technology in your home and staying in charge probably won't be easy. You will be swimming against the tide, and you may get criticism from your extended family (especially if your child's grandparents believe that love equals indulgence), maybe from other parents at the school gates, maybe even from your closest friends. On the other hand, your family and friends may be cheering you on, and they may want to learn from you how to get back in charge.

Staying consistent will be difficult at times. Humans are not by nature very good at being consistent; we change our minds and our plans a lot. And getting back in charge can feel like hard work, for one thing because dealing with our children's initial fury about the new screen time rules and routines can be very upsetting. You may feel frustrated, angry, guilty, confused. You may feel like giving up. You will need to keep your wits about you; you won't be able to let your guard down. That can feel exhausting at first, until the new routines are firmly established.

Parenting as a journey is a popular metaphor. A journey has a starting point and a destination. For the parents who are reading this book, the starting point is that you're not completely happy with what is happening with electronics in your home: your child is too much in charge and your values are not prevailing. You won't reach your destination in one giant leap. You'll be taking lots of small steps. And to complicate matters, you and your partner may be at different points in this journey towards getting back in charge.

Let me conclude this chapter by reminding you of what's possible when you use the Calmer, Easier, Happier Parenting strategies. Screen time problems will be significantly reduced, and most can be eliminated. Even a severe problem can be transformed. Soon it will become a moderate issue, and then it will become a mild issue. Eventually, with consistency, it will end up a very mild issue. That is probably the best result you can hope for, given that our children will always be surrounded by the influences of Screen World. But you can live with a very mild issue because your children's objections will fade over time. Your children and teens will find renewed pleasure in non-screen activities. You will get more cooperation and respect. You will see more self-reliance and responsibility. You will have the immense satisfaction of seeing your children and teens developing more mature values and habits. This book can give you the tools to make all this happen.

Children and teens

You will notice that in this book I frequently use the phrase 'children and teens'. It may feel to you that it doesn't make sense to lump together such a wide age range. You may be convinced that what works for children won't work for teens. You may feel that teens are very different from younger children and even from preteens who are only a few years younger.

In some ways this is true. Particularly in affluent, largely urban countries like ours, what's different about modern teens, compared to younger children, is that many teens want to be treated as adults; they believe they should have the freedom to make decisions for themselves. But it's clear to parents and teachers that teens are not even close to being mature adults. They still need plenty of teaching and training.

Another thing that is different is that the scathing attitude of many teens, especially when you start getting back in charge of electronics, can easily undermine a parent's confidence. Especially when it comes to screen use, parents tend to vacillate between two poles. One extreme is often called 'backing off', which usually means trying not to nag, lecture or tell off, trying to say nothing about screen excesses and accompanying rudeness. Parents do this partly because this is what many professionals seem to advise, and also because they are nervous about how their teen would react if they were to put their foot down.

But sooner or later the strain of trying to be patient while you see your values being ignored becomes too stressful to bear. Then parents find themselves nagging, telling off, threatening, possibly shouting. Neither extreme feels good to the parent, and neither extreme is effective at guiding children or teens to develop more mature screen habits.

In Chapter 5 I address some of the worrying trends that teens and preteens are increasingly having to deal with in Screen World: cyber bullying, cyberchondria, plagiarism, gambling, sexting and pornography. Many books have been written about these deeply upsetting issues, detailing the negative impact on teens and their families. In this book, particularly in Sections Two and Three, I offer some guidelines for helping teens navigate their way through these murky waters.

Thankfully, one thing that is the same about children and teens is that the strategies I teach in this book will work to develop more sensible habits in both. It may take longer with teenagers, and there may be a few more unpleasant scenes along the way, but you can achieve your goals.

CHAPTER 2
THE FOUR SCREEN ISSUES

Screen time issues fall into four major categories.

A **How much** time your children and teens spend in front of a screen

A huge worry and source of guilt for many parents is the amount of time, on a typical day, their children are sitting in front of a screen. Parents feel, intuitively, that it is too much, but they are confused and don't know who to listen to – their children, their gut feeling or the experts.

The more time children are on a screen, the more likely it is that certain problems will develop (I explore these problems in the next two chapters). But children can be very persuasive, and parental peer pressure (what parents believe that other parents allow their children to do) can lead you to doubt your own judgement.

And the experts often disagree amongst themselves too. One of the appealing features of the internet is that if you search long enough, you are bound to come across an expert who agrees with you. So you can't rely on the experts. You still have to decide about screen issues for yourself, based on your values and also on what you know your children can comfortably handle.

How can you find out how much time your child spends in front of a screen? You may be able to find out simply by asking him. How willingly and how honestly he will share his screen life with you depends on a number of factors, including his age, his temperament, the influence of his peer group, and also how well you and he get on most of the time. You can't count on him to tell you the whole truth if he knows you disapprove.

You might be able to find out the answer to this question by being more observant. You will probably need to jot down what you observe as memories are often not reliable. This will also minimise arguments between you and your partner if you each have differing perceptions of what your children are actually doing in their leisure time.

But children can be clever about disguising their screen time. You may be assuming your child is doing her homework, but as you walk in the room the screen suddenly switches back to her essay. Or your child is texting in the loo or after bedtime under the covers. This secretiveness is most likely to happen when parents have inadvertently turned screen time into a battle zone by telling off, threatening, blaming and predicting a dire future of exam failure and a career as a street sweeper.

The older children get, the less time they spend with us, so we can't see what they are doing. Once teens or preteens are allowed to bring their mobiles to school, we can safely assume they will be using them whenever possible: at lunch time, at breaks between lessons, and even during lessons if the teachers are willing to overlook it. Too many teachers have given up trying to control mobile use. This is because too many schools don't put sensible guidelines in place, or don't monitor the problem closely or don't follow through consistently when rules are broken or bent.

Here are the current averages for Britain:

- Children of **three and four years old** typically are in front of a screen for **three hours a day**.

- By the time children are **five to seven years old**, the average is **four hours a day**.
- Between **eight and eleven years old**, the average has risen slightly, to **four-and-a-half hours a day**.
- The average for **teens** is **six-and-a-half hours a day**.

Compare this with the British Medical Association guidelines:

- **Birth to age two** – **no exposure to screens at all**.
- **Ages two to five years** – a maximum of **one hour a day** leisure screen use.
- Ages **five to eighteen years** – a maximum of **two hours a day**.

As you will see in the next few pages, the Calmer, Easier, Happier Parenting recommendations are more stringent than this. But ultimately it is up to each of us to decide, based on our values, how much screen time we think is right for each of our children.

The Calmer, Easier, Happier Parenting guidelines:

- **Under 3 years old** – even though the current guidelines say no screen activity before age two, I ask parents to extend the **ban on all screen exposure** to three years old. This recommendation is based on research, parents' reports, and on my own observation of how screen use adversely affects toddlers' moods, concentration, confidence and resilience.

Below the age of three years, screen use can be detrimental. So my guidelines about content are for children three years old and above. But let me start by addressing the fact that many children below this age do spend a considerable amount of time in front of screens.

Nowadays toddlers are likely to be watching television, playing simple games on a tablet or on a parent's phone, usually with cartoon characters. You may want to defend the use of screens below the ages of two or three years old by pointing out that on-screen games for toddlers teach letters, numbers, colours, animal sounds, etc. All the evidence tells us that toddlers learn these concepts and facts at the same age if an adult is willing to play with them regularly. There is no added benefit to toddlers learning via a screen.

At this point you may feel like arguing that parents need a break from a toddler's incessant demands and interruptions and surely a bit of screen time won't be harmful? This parent spoke for many when she explained why she put her eight-month-old daughter in a bouncy seat in front of a Baby Einstein-type video every evening:

> *It gives me and my husband a twenty-minute break. We can have dinner in peace and catch up on our day without being interrupted. When she's whingeing because she wants us to pay attention to her, we feel guilty if we ignore her. This way she's happy so we can relax.*

What parent doesn't want some guilt-free downtime every day? In the days before the Square Nanny, parents learned to disregard babies' and children's fussing, their whims and wants (but obviously not their real needs) for periods of time every day. As a result, young children, even babies, soon grew comfortable entertaining themselves for longer and longer stretches of time. Quite quickly they started developing the essential life skills of self-reliance, confidence, resilience, patience, flexibility, problem-solving, independence and self-soothing.

In many families this habit has largely faded away. Widespread reliance on screens to entertain and distract our children is one reason why more children nowadays are perceived by parents and teachers to be sensitive, clingy, unconfident and inflexible.

It's true that a bit of screen time won't harm your baby or toddler, but before too long what started out as a bit of screen time becomes a bit more and a bit more and a bit more. That's because screen time is so addictive. And using electronics to keep children quiet can easily become a habit that parents come to rely on.

In Section Three I will show you how to guide your children, even toddlers, into the habit of playing contentedly by themselves, without needing input from an adult. This will significantly reduce the annoying demands and interruptions so you will be much less tempted to use electronics as a sedative.

Of course, with a first child or an only child it's easier to stick to my 'No screens under age three' guideline. A second child is likely to be exposed to the older sibling's screen use long before the age of three. But we can do a lot to minimise the toddler's screen exposure.

- **From three to eight years old** – you may not like my guidelines for this age group! I recommend that between the ages of three and eight years old, leisure screen time be limited to a maximum of **half an hour a day**. This doesn't mean half an hour of television and half an hour of Wii and a half an hour of playing on your phone, etc. I'm talking about a total of half an hour of leisure screen use per day. If your child needs (not just wants) to do his homework or revision on a screen, that's separate. And of course there's no law that says a child has to have screen time every day. After all, there are very few other leisure activities that children do every day.

  Educational apps have become very popular. They still count as leisure screen use unless <u>you</u> decide they're important for your child to do. Do keep in mind that online educational games are rarely as effective at teaching skills, facts and concepts as one-on-one time with a parent or other caregiver.

  If the thought of limiting leisure screen time to half an hour a day for this age group fills you with dread, read on. You <u>can</u> get back in charge of the screens in your home, and everyone will feel better for it.

- **From eight years old throughout adulthood** – for children and teens, and for many adults as well, screen time has become the default activity when no other entertainment or distraction is on offer. As a result, children and teens gradually lose interest in the wholesome, constructive pastimes and hobbies they used to enjoy.

My recommendation from age eight upwards is a maximum of an hour per day of leisure screen time. That figure is based on my experience of how the human body and brain react to leisure screen use. If your child needs to use the computer for homework, that's completely separate from leisure screen use.

Limiting leisure screen time to one hour a day may seem just about doable during the week, when many children's afternoons and evenings are taken up with extracurricular activities, homework, music practice and maybe playdates. But limiting screen time to one hour a day at weekends and on holidays may feel harsh, especially if you believe that children need to be entertained. The strategies I teach in this book will show you how to help children and teens cope with and thrive on significantly less screen time than they've been accustomed to. And of course you can make occasional exceptions. I talk about that in my Q & As in Chapter 12.

If your child is currently racking up many more hours than this, don't despair. Any reduction is likely to improve the negative effects of too much electronics. I advocate gradual (but not slow) cutting back, rather that cold turkey. This way you minimise the shock to the system and the resulting emotional discomfort, which can include anxiety (and sometimes even depression) as well as resentment.

In Chapter 8 I offer suggestions for how to limit the amount of screen time. All of my recommendations have been tried and tested by real parents who started

out unsure and anxious, just as you may be feeling now.
These parents gradually felt stronger and more confident as they experienced for themselves the positive
effects of drastically reducing the amount of screen time
in their families.

Having screens on in the background

Parents may excuse the amount of screen time a child is
exposed to because the television or video is on in the background while the child is playing, and the child is not paying
much attention to what's on the screen. Unfortunately,
even exposure to background screens is not good for children – or for adults, for that matter.

Here is what I observed during a home consultation.
The child, aged five, was absorbed in making a building
out of Lego, apparently paying no attention to the cartoon
on the screen, while his mother and I sat chatting. His
concentration on what he was creating and his obvious
enjoyment were delightful to watch. When his father came
home a little while later and asked his son, *'What have you
been doing?'* the boy replied, *'Watching TV'*, even though
he had barely glanced at the cartoon. The boy's experience
was defined not by the pleasure of creating, but by the
huge screen, the manic cartoon characters, the loud, silly
voices, the garish colours.

Having a screen on in the background when no one is
focused on it gets children accustomed to the constant
presence of screens. After a while silence starts to feel odd
and uncomfortable. It feels as if the silence needs to be
filled – by a screen. Being in front of a screen becomes the
norm.

B **What** they are doing, and what values are they being exposed to

Games (on computers, laptops, mobile phones and other hand-held devices)

Creating and building games

These games, such as Minecraft, can be very constructive, teaching problem-solving skills and expanding children's imagination. If these are the sorts of games your child is drawn to, you may feel so relieved about their choice of screen activity that you don't pay too much attention to how many hours she is on the screen. Remember that the guidelines for the amount of screen time apply even if you are completely happy with the content. That's because there are unwelcome effects from too much screen time, quite apart from the content and quality of what's on the screen.

Games involving aggression (destruction of property and killing)

There are mixed opinions about screen aggression and screen violence. There are a few experts who claim that watching or interacting with aggressive activities on the screen does no harm and may in fact be helpful at channelling aggressive impulses harmlessly. Most research however demonstrates a link between watching or participating in on-screen aggression and heightened aggression and anxiety in real life. The link is not always obvious because the real-life aggression can take a number of different forms, including more disrespect towards parents, more teasing of younger siblings, more impulsive lashing out or shouting when frustrated, less cooperation at home.

What seems to be happening is that the on-screen

aggression triggers the release of certain chemicals in the brain, which produce feelings of aggression or anxiety (or both at the same time), and the brain has to do something with those feelings. The way those feelings come out often does not seem connected in terms of content with the on-screen aggression that provoked it. Similarly, the anxiety that is triggered by on-screen aggression or violence can take many seemingly unrelated forms, such as fear of the dark, worrying about burglars and worrying about global catastrophes.

You can do your own in-house experiment, as many parents have done. If you have a child or teen who spends an hour or more a day watching or participating in on-screen aggression, you can reduce this amount to one or two hours a week and notice for yourself the result. Parents regularly report that within a few weeks their child's anger and resentment fade significantly, and he becomes much calmer, smilier and more cooperative. Anxieties will also fade, and he will become braver and more emotionally resilient.

Games that focus on violence and destruction are especially popular with boys because of their higher levels of testosterone, as well as their conditioning. As much as we might like to at times, we can't wave a magic wand that will remove from a boy's make-up the fascination with power and competition and strength and winning, with exploding and maiming and destroying.

With some boys, this tendency is so strong that if unchecked they would play aggressive computer games for many hours a day. Usually these are the boys who have a more extreme temperament; compared to other boys their age they are more active, sensitive, intense, impulsive, inflexible and immature. Unfortunately, the games that focus on killing and destroying tend to exacerbate these characteristics.

A boy may drive you mad pleading for 18+ games, hoping to convince you that all his friends' parents are OK with it, and that you're the only parents in the world who are so old-fashioned and controlling. And many parents do end up giving in to the pestering. Despite their moral objections, they ignore the age recommendations that come with games.

But there are two very important reasons not to allow a child access to games designed for 18+. Even middle-teens are not emotionally equipped to deal with 18+ computer games, especially because the graphics nowadays are so lifelike. For example, the blood spurting from wounds looks very realistic. This realism blurs the line, emotionally, between fantasy and reality. A teen's habits and values are still in flux, so he is very easily influenced.

Also, and this cannot be emphasised strongly enough, when children and teens see parents ignoring government recommendations, this sets a very bad example. It leads children to lose respect for the law and also to lose respect for the parents who allow themselves to be persuaded.

Below the age of eight, children should be shielded from these aggressive games. That includes passively watching while an older sibling plays these games. But from the age of eight upwards, I don't suggest that you impose a blanket ban on all games that feature killing. That is likely to cause huge resentment, and a small amount won't be harmful. If your child loves these aggressive games, I suggest limiting them to a few days a week, with a day or two off in between. Having a few days a week when he is not playing these games will lessen their addictive hold on him, or even prevent that fixation from developing in the first place. If you want to know how to make your rules stick, the strategies in Sections Two and Three will help.

Fantasy sports
This term refers to any sports competition that has imaginary online teams. The activity consists of owning, adding to, managing and coaching your team. The games are based on statistics from real players or teams. There are positive aspects to these games, and it's an activity that boys often share with their fathers. We need to make sure it doesn't replace fathers and sons doing real things together.

Learning games
These games, which usually focus on literacy, numeracy or problem-solving skills, are not usually a child's first choice of computer games. But if parents make the decision that educational games are the only computer games on offer, children will usually jump at the chance. But let's remember that the actual learning that takes place is often minimal.

Communicating with peers via mobile phones
Mobile phones are so versatile that it's no wonder that children at younger and younger ages are fascinated by them and become dependent on them.

One important use of mobiles is to make plans to meet up. In the pre-technology past, when telephones were fixed in one spot, getting together with friends had to be planned in advance. Most of us can remember a time before mobiles, when we didn't have a way of changing our plans at the last minute so we had to stick with what had been decided. But now, with instant communication via mobiles, plans can, and often do, change from minute to minute. This is a major reason why young people feel so lost without their phones. What if your friends who were going to be at a certain place at a certain time suddenly decide to go somewhere else? Without a mobile, it's easy to get left out. One disadvantage of mobile phones is that they remove the need for young people to think ahead, so they do not become practised at it. One result is that in terms of taking responsibility, they stay at an immature level.

Mobiles are also used for posting comments during and after get-togethers. In fact a number of parents have reported their pre-teen (usually a girl) and her friends texting one another when they're all in the same room!

Mobile phones have reinforced society's view of parents as servants. Parents end up at their child's beck and call, not only when they are with their child but wherever the child happens to be. Parents regularly get texts about issues that feel like emergencies to the child or teen: *'Will you pick me up from school today because I'm not going home with Tracy because she was mean to me.'*

I recommend that parents make a rule that plans that involve the parent are arranged in the morning and they only change if there is a real emergency, and the parent is the person who decides what constitutes an emergency. Without this rule, your children and teens won't be getting practice at impulse-control. They will not be learning how to think carefully about possible consequences before they make decisions.

At what age should my child be allowed a mobile phone?

The trend is to buy children mobile phones at younger and younger ages or to let them have a cast-off when a parent or older sibling gets a newer model. This is mostly driven by pester power, but parents may also believe that this is how they can keep their child safe when he's not with them. This reasoning ignores several important facts.

Statistically, our children are safer than ever before. Also, we need to be teaching them skills for keeping themselves safe. And while they're on their phones, which are really mini-computers, they are not safe from negative influences online. And once a child owns a mobile, he will probably want to be on it a lot!

I recommend parents hold off giving their child a mobile phone until the start of secondary school. They should also make sure to disable as many of the computer functions as possible so that the mobile phone really is just a phone.

Social media, online chatrooms and forums

Teens, preteens and even younger children are using social media, usually accessed via mobile phones, to keep tabs on what their friends and acquaintances (and enemies) are doing and thinking. They also post photographs and comments designed to impress their friends and acquaintances (and once again, their enemies) with how great their life is or how terrible their parents or teachers (or enemies) are. The comments can get nasty because there's no live feedback to force young people to see how what they are saying is affecting others. The strategies in this book will help guide your children and teens to be kinder and more civilised in their interactions with peers, both online and offline.

Participating in online chatrooms and forums can be a very positive experience, enabling young people to communicate with others who share their interests. Unsupervised it can be very negative. They might be with online 'friends' whom they've never met face-to-face and about whom they and you know nothing. Most children know the rules about internet safety but regularly ignore them. We've all read about young people who were tricked into meeting in person someone they had 'met' and become friends with online, someone who gained their trust, someone who complimented and flattered them – with tragic consequences.

You may be sure your child isn't doing this sort of thing because you have access to her social media accounts. Maybe she's 'friended' you on Facebook. Be warned: children, especially teens, share information with each other about how to get round parental controls and parental monitoring. One very common way is to have one Facebook or Instagram account that parents have access to and one account that the parents don't even know exists.

Watching television programmes and films (not only on a television, but also on laptops, tablets and mobile phones)

These can be very enriching or a waste of time or actually damaging.

Research has shown that children and teens imitate what they see on their screens. Many films and television programmes aimed at children, preteens and teens get their laughs by portraying adults as bumbling idiots: old-fashioned, clueless, easy to manipulate, trying too hard to be liked – in short, uncool. On screen, children and teens are cleverer than adults, skilled at getting their way, devious, very persuasive.

These programmes and films are fiction so of course we expect our children to understand and remember that real life is not like this. On one level they do know this, but on a deeper level they are influenced by what they see on a screen. These characters and their antics give children and teens very vivid templates for what to say, how to react and behave, and it's natural for young people to imitate what they see and hear. These fictional characters and scenarios erode respect for parents and teachers.

If you make the time to watch with your children, you will be able to talk with them about the values they are being exposed to. In Chapter 16 I suggest a strategy called Reflective Listening that will help children and teens to open up about their beliefs and feelings and to be more ready to listen when you talk about your beliefs and feelings.

Positive uses of technology

Taking photographs, writing blogs and stories, making videos and vlogs, 'painting', coding
These are all active, creative uses of technology. However, you will still need to monitor the amount of time they absorb.

Reading on e-readers
Electronic readers can make the experience of reading more palatable for children or teens who are not yet fluent, confident readers. First of all, just the fact that the book is on an electronic device will probably make the activity of reading a bit more appealing. In addition, your child can enlarge the font size and make wider spaces between lines of print, both of which will make the text easier to read. Conventional books consist of black print on white paper, which produces a disturbing glare for many reluctant readers. But e-readers can have an off-white background, which reduces the contrast and is more restful for the eyes.

E-readers may also contain a feature that can actually improve reading skills. If the device includes an audio recording of the book, this is ideal. When the words of the story are entering the brain via two sensory channels, the auditory as well as the visual, this maximises learning, both understanding and retention.

Surfing the web (searching for information in print, images or videos on topics of interest)

Children often use the internet to find out more about school subjects that interest them. As they get older, they're likely to be searching for things to do with pop culture: fashion, celebrities, music, sports, sex and romance, diets, friendships and, of course, electronics.

There are pros and cons to allowing children to surf the web. Of course, we want children to be curious, to be excited about learning. And the more children learn, the more they want to learn. Sometimes children and teens become passionate about a subject through exploring it on the internet.

But due to the addictive nature of technology, surfing the web can easily expand to fill far too many hours of your child's life, hours better spent playing sports, hanging out with friends, pursuing hobbies, participating in family activities.

A lot of the information on the web is opinion dressed up as fact. Numerous experiments have shown that even teens who seem to be well-informed and mature are easily taken in by the authoritative tone of the 'experts' they find on the internet.

A new word has been coined, cyberchondria, defined as an unfounded anxiety about one's physical or emotional health, brought on by visiting multiple health and medical websites. This problem affects children and teens as well as adults. They can convince themselves that they are the victim of an exotic medical condition. Teens in particular may embrace a 'diagnosis', especially if it gives them a ready explanation for the malaise they may be feeling.

Screens v. real life

Because screen time so easily expands to fill more and more unscheduled leisure time, children and teens gradually lose interest in the activities that are good for their bodies, brains and emotions. I regularly ask parents this question:

'What do you wish your children and teens were doing more of, instead of being glued to a screen?' Here's how parents answer this question:

Spending time with siblings and parents

Spending time with friends

Playing outside

Reading

Sports and other exercise

Pursuing hobbies they've neglected, e.g. arts and crafts, building and modelling, music

Helping around the house

Homework and revision

In Sections Two and Three I explain how parents can guide their children and teens to participate more in real life.

Internet filters

Young people are more knowledgeable than their parents about things like internet filters. I recently read about a school that took the obvious precaution of blocking certain sites on their new school computers. It took the students less than half an hour of experimenting to discover that they could access all the forbidden sites simply by searching in Spanish rather than in English. Children and teens display amazing ingenuity and perseverance when it comes to making sure they get their daily dose of screen activity.

We need to use all the tools available to limit not only the amount of time our kids spend in front of a screen, but also what they are exposed to and what they do in front of the screen. But we cannot rely on our ability to do this. In addition, we need to guide our children and teens to become more willing to engage in the activities that we think are good for them. We can foster this willingness by using a number of the strategies that I introduce in Section Three.

C <u>When</u> they're on a screen – what times of day (and night)

Here's a scary statistic: research carried out in the US reveals that on average teenagers send and receive more than 200 texts a day, the first one before they even get out of bed in the morning and the last one after midnight, long after parents assume they are asleep.

It's easy to dismiss this report because here in the UK we tend to think of the US as a land of excess; we assume that the same sorts of things couldn't happen here. Sadly, the UK is not far behind the US in its tech habits.

Early mornings

Many children eat their breakfast in front of a screen. Or they are allowed some screen time as a reward for getting dressed without dawdling.

I recommend no screen time before school. Similarly, no screens on weekends and holidays until homework, revision and music practice are completed. This is because most screen use tends to reinforce impulsivity and distractibility. These are the opposite mental states to the focus and self-control anyone needs in order to absorb and remember new information and skills and to challenge oneself to do one's best.

Mealtimes

Meals are the ideal time for family members to reconnect every day. We can start our mornings earlier so that we build in enough time to have a relaxing breakfast with our children; this goes a long way towards setting everyone up to have a good (or at least better) day. At dinner we can come together to share the highs and lows of our day. Any screen activity during mealtimes will interfere with this.

Night-time

Parenting experts and the medical profession agree that children and teens are not getting enough sleep. Electronics too close to bedtime and after bedtime are not the only causes of this epidemic, but this is a major contributing factor.

Screens keep children and teens occupied and out of mischief so it's easy for parents to get absorbed in their own tasks and not realise that it's already past bedtime. By then the children are likely to be overtired, wired, and complaining loudly when told to get off the screen and go to bed. Many children are in the habit of resisting bedtime. Being expected to go straight from a screen into the bedtime routine can make the transition to bed even less welcome.

The blue-ish light emitted by electronics suppresses the production of melatonin, the brain chemical that makes us sleepy. Being in front of a screen within two hours of bedtime can cause sleep disturbances. This might be difficulty in drifting off to sleep even though tired, or waking in the night and not being able to get back to sleep easily, or waking too early, or waking in the morning still feeling tired. The current guideline is that all screens should be switched off about two hours before lights out.

In case you're wondering how to make this happen in your family, you're not alone. Children are not born knowing that they should do what we tell them to do (cooperation). They're also not born knowing that they should remember what we've told them in the past and do it today without our having to tell them yet again (self-reliance). Cooperation and self-reliance are habits that children and teens learn most easily and best when we take the time to teach them. This is much more effective than simply expecting them to do things right and then getting annoyed with them when they don't. If you're not sure how to teach and train the important skills of cooperation and self-reliance, read on. In Section Three I explain some useful strategies for teaching and training children and young people who seem resistant.

D **Where** they are when they're on their screens

Every article about electronics tells parents not to let children and teenagers have computers and televisions in their bedrooms, and yet the habit is becoming more and more prevalent and with younger and younger children. Here I will talk about why this rule is so important, and later in the book I will explain what parents can do to reverse this situation if you have already allowed your teenager to have a computer or a television or any electronic device in his bedroom.

It stands to reason that the more accessible screens are, the more our children will be on them. Electronic equipment in bedrooms of course leads to more screen use. And allowing teens to have screens in their bedrooms legitimises being in front of a screen as an activity that parents are not only endorsing and approving of but even encouraging.

It also leads to teens and preteens spending more time alone in their rooms, isolating themselves from the rest of the family, isolated from the family's values. Often this is unintentional; the lure of the electronics is just too strong to resist. But choosing to isolate oneself can become a habit, especially when being with the family involves being lectured and criticised. It's quite understandable that a child or teen would want to escape from those unpleasant interactions into a different world.

And when kids are in their bedroom, usually with the door closed, parents do not know what they are up to, what sites they are accessing, who they are 'chatting' to, what ideas and values they are being exposed to.

Screens in bedrooms are also a recipe for sleep deprivation. Studies have shown that young people who have electronic equipment in their bedroom spend significantly fewer hours asleep. Unfortunately, one of the results of this sleep deprivation is lethargy and a lack of energy, which makes spending time in front of a screen even more attractive. Isolation from family, combined with sleep deprivation, make young people more vulnerable, not only to negative influences, but also to mental health issues such as anxiety and depression.

If at present there are no screens in your child's or teenager's bedroom, please keep it that way, no matter how much they plead, pester and try to convince you. If, however, your teens already have screens in their bedrooms and you want to reverse this, it is possible. It probably won't be easy, but it is well worth the effort. When screens come out of your child's or teen's bedroom he will spend more time with his family, more time doing homework and revising, more time interacting with the real world. But parents are sometimes scared to make this change because they have seen that screen dependency leads children and teens to react negatively, with verbal and sometimes even physical aggression.

If you insist that all screens be kept in the communal parts of the home, you will be able to monitor how much time your children and teens are on screens. You will also be able to notice any inappropriate content – in theory. But even the most cooperative children and teens can become very sneaky if they are driven by screen dependency to break rules and guidelines. Because of the addictive pull of electronics, keeping an eye on what's happening on the screen will often not be enough. Most children and teenagers (and many adults as well) don't have the self-control necessary to temporarily deny themselves the good feeling that comes from screen use. So in most families keeping an eye on what's happening on the screen is just the beginning. Frequent and unpredictable monitoring will be necessary, even if you're in the same room where the screens are.

You may be wondering at what age teenagers have the maturity to make sensible decisions about screens in their bedrooms. My reply may seem hopelessly old-fashioned and unrealistic. Instead of worrying about some magic age of maturity, I recommend having a blanket rule: no screens in bedrooms, regardless of age or maturity – and that includes parents.

CHAPTER 3
HOW BIG IS YOUR FAMILY'S PROBLEM?

In case you're not sure how important the screen time issues you're dealing with really are, here is a questionnaire that may help you to gain some perspective. I've divided the screen issues into four categories:

- **Absolutely no problems** This is very rare once your child is past the age of four or five years old.
- **Mild problems** This is the category I suggest you aim for. As children get older, dealing with such a powerful mood-altering activity as electronics will never again be completely trouble-free. This category is quite rare nowadays. But when you take a positive, firm and consistent approach to screen time, this category of mild problems is completely achievable, even during the teen years.
- **Moderate/typical problems** This is the category that many families fall into nowadays. Please remember that even though this is typical, it doesn't have to be this way.
- **Severe problems** This category is becoming increasingly common, especially if you have a teenager.

For each of these categories, I've listed below some examples of screen behaviours. You may not agree with how I've drawn up these lists. I may have put a particular screen behaviour into the category of **moderate/typical problems**, but maybe you've become so accustomed to that problem that by now it feels like a **mild problem** that you just have to put up with.

When you read the following examples, I want you to keep referring back to your values and to your goals for your children. Don't assume you have to put up with anything that doesn't feel right to you. Identify the screen behaviour that you would like to see less of, and then keep reading to learn more about how you can improve these worrying or annoying habits.

Absolutely no problems

Examples:

- Your child enjoys screen time while it's happening, but she switches off without a fuss as soon as she is told to.
- Your child knows when he can and can't have screen time so he rarely asks for it at other times.
- Siblings play well together most of the time so you're not tempted to use screen time to keep things calm.
- Your child plays contentedly with his friends (most of the time), without asking for screen time.
- Your child plays by himself for some time every day, enjoying a variety of non-screen activities.
- Your child or teen listens when you explain the rules and routines surrounding screen use: how much, what it can be, when, where, why, etc. He understands and accepts with good grace that you are the parents and you make the rules.
- Your teenager is very sensible about prioritising home-work, revision, music practice and household responsibilities before leisure screen use. You never worry.

Mild problems

Examples:

- Your child knows when he can and cannot have his screen time, and mostly sticks to your rules, but he asks for it at other times more often than you would like. He accepts the rules with a little arguing or whingeing.
- If given the opportunity, your child will delay coming off a screen when her time is up. She may argue half-heartedly, but she complies (although not as quickly as you would like).
- Your child usually follows the screen rules and routines, partly from habit and partly because he knows you're monitoring consistently. When you forget to be vigilant, you can expect him to notice and to take advantage. He'll see what he can get away with.

Moderate/typical problems

Examples:

- In theory your child knows when he can and cannot have his screen time, but he often begs or pesters for it at other times (probably because a parent or caregiver has been inconsistent).
- Your child expects to be able to play on your tablet or mobile phone when he has to wait or when what's happening around him doesn't interest him, eg
  - in restaurants
  - on car journeys
  - in waiting rooms

- when adults are talking amongst themselves and not paying attention to him

- If your mobile phone is lying on the table, your child may pick it up and start playing with it without asking your permission.

- If you haven't seen your child in a while and you go looking for him, you may well find him in front of a screen in another part of the house or flat.

- More often than you would like, your child makes a big fuss when it's time to come off the screen: prolonged arguing, complaining or pleading, possibly shouting.

- Your child is so immersed in Screen World that he may not even look up or respond when you talk to him. If he does answer, it may be a surly grunt, with his eyes still on the screen.

- If you confiscate your child's laptop or hand-held device or mobile, it's not too long before you find him on another screen. In many homes there are a number of no-longer-exciting devices lying around; the children have forgotten about them – until the latest model is not available.

- Your child, or more likely your teen, has multiple screens on at the same time. She may be texting on her phone and surfing YouTube on her laptop or tablet while half-watching a film or programme on the television. Multi-screening is one reason why the average number of screen hours for teenagers is so high.

- Sending and receiving texts from friends and checking social media intrudes into family activities, meals and conversations.

- You find yourself using screens to distract your toddler so that you can get him dressed without a fuss.

- Your children complain, argue or plead when you first make rules about screen time.

- Your child manages to convince you or your partner to let him have more screen time than you feel is right.
- Your children ignore the rules, hoping that you will be too preoccupied to notice or remember.
- If you're not vigilant, your child will sneak a device under the covers and use it after lights out.
- If he can get away with it, your child will choose screen time over family time or playing outdoors, but he will join in non-screen activities when you insist, and he will enjoy himself (although he may not want to admit it).
- Your child assumes that no friend will want to come round unless they can be on a screen for the whole of the playdate.
- Your children are delighted when the stricter or more vigilant parent is away from home as that means they can have lots more screen time.

When you have **moderate/typical problems**, a vicious circle can develop. Parents don't make clear rules about screen time, or else they make rules but don't follow through consistently (in Chapter 7 I explore why parents have such a hard time following through with screen rules). As a result, children take advantage, pushing the boundaries. Parents react by nagging or threatening. Children complain and argue. Parents, feeling powerless, nag even more. Children resist even more. This cycle of negativity can seriously undermine the parent-child relationship.

Severe problems

Examples:

- Your children or teens are very angry about the new rules because they can't really imagine what their life will be like if they can't have the amount of screen time they're currently used to. Their reaction is over the top and often very disrespectful:

'You're ruining my life.'

'This is child abuse.'

- Your child or teen is on a device after midnight.
- You child or teen has managed to convince you to let him have screens in his bedroom.
- Your child goes into your handbag without your permission to get your phone. He may not even bother to do this surreptitiously if in the past parents haven't taken consistent action to prevent it.
- A child stays awake until the parents are asleep and then creeps into the sitting room to use the computer.
- Your child or teen won't invite friends round because your electronic equipment is outdated and uncool.
- Your child repeatedly breaks the rules: bringing phones to the dinner table, refusing to hand over the laptop or phone (or dongle or lead etc.) when her screen time is up.
- Your child has huge emotional reactions to screen limits, or even just to hearing you talk about screen limits. A young child may sob inconsolably, scream or have a full-scale tantrum.
- Your child may react to new rules or routines with verbal aggression: insulting, swearing, blaming, threatening or screaming.
- Your child may become physically aggressive when you try to switch off or confiscate a device. As well as arguing, shouting and not letting go, he may push, hit or kick.
- A child or teen who is angry about a screen time rule or consequence may stop short of overt physical

aggression, but he may subtly intimidate you, standing too close as he shouts or pushing past you roughly.
- Your teen spends more and more time outside of the house or holed up in his bedroom.
- Your teen is gambling online.
- Your teen is sending or receiving sexually explicit images or texts (sexting).

You can congratulate yourself if most of the screen behaviours you're dealing with fall into the **absolutely no problems** or **mild problems** categories. But be warned that it will take commitment on your part to keep your family in one of these categories. If your children are still young, you may have a hard time believing that screen time could ever become a big problem. But as your children grow they will inevitably be exposed, outside the home, to other influences, and they are bound to be affected. So don't just wait until that happens; prepare yourself. Learn some strategies to help you stay in charge and to guide your growing children into wholesome and sensible screen habits.

On the other hand, you may be dismayed by some of these examples. You may not have realised how bad things had got. Please don't feel discouraged if many of your family's screen issues fall into the categories of **moderate/typical problems** or **severe problems**. It's never too late to get back in charge, and this book is packed full of ideas for how to improve the screen situation in your home.

CHAPTER 4

THE NEGATIVE EFFECTS OF SCREEN TIME

Everything that we do has an effect on us, physically, mentally and emotionally. Some activities leave us feeling relaxed, energised, satisfied, excited, proud of ourselves, able to think clearly. Other activities can leave us feeling stressed, drained, frustrated, disappointed, confused, annoyed with ourselves and with life. The same is true for our children. Every aspect of their lifestyle affects them.

The basics of a child's or teen's lifestyle are nutrition, sleep, exercise and balancing their work (usually school, homework, revision and contributing to the household) with their leisure (which includes enjoyable time spent with family and friends, and also pastimes such as after-school activities, playing and time in front of a screen). Of course we want to provide our children with a lifestyle that will bring out the best in them, in the present and for the future.

Screen time is the aspect of our children's lifestyle that parents nowadays worry about the most and often feel powerless to do anything about. Our children are affected by every aspect of electronics: how much screen time they have, what they are doing in front of a screen, when and where they do it and with whom. All of these factors will influence a child's mood, her behaviour, what she thinks about herself and her family, her friends and her teachers.

In this chapter I will explain how screen habits adversely affect the other elements of a child's lifestyle. I will outline the negative or problematic effects on children's bodies, brains, emotions and behaviour of their screen time. This won't make for comfortable reading; it's depressing and worrying. That's all the more reason to be determined to get back in charge. In case you assume from this catalogue of negative effects that I am against screens, let me repeat here that there are positive aspects to a variety of screen activities, as long as the four screen issues (how many hours each day, what type of content, when and where) are addressed sensibly.

How too much screen time affects our children's bodies

Quite apart from the content of screen activity, the amount of time children spend in front of a screen has an impact on their food choices and eating habits, on the amount of exercise they take and on their levels of fitness.

- **Humans have evolved over millennia to be active for a large part of every day, and we evolved to learn by doing.**
  Embedded in our DNA, the childhood of our ancient ancestors remains the template for how our children's bodies and brains function best. When they are in front of a screen they are not moving their bodies, not burning off calories (unless they are playing Wii Sports). The more hours in a day they aren't moving much, the more likely they are to be overweight or 'underfit'.

  Television pumps out round-the-clock news of crimes against children, and parents understandably react by keeping children close, even though the statistics tell us that children are safer than in the past. But worried parents are not taking any chances; they are keeping children indoors. The latest surveys show that many children spend ninety percent of their waking hours indoors. This is very different from a generation ago, when children in the country roamed far and wide, and children in the city played outside on the pavement or in the street for hours after school.

When children are stuck indoors, underfoot, interrupting you when you're trying to get things done, their natural exuberance and curiosity can be very irritating. So it's not surprising that parents have come to rely on the 'electronic sedative' to maintain a semblance of order. This sedentary, screen-based childhood contributes to obesity, which is on the rise. The latest statistics reveal that almost twenty percent of four and five year olds are overweight and about thirty percent of ten and eleven year olds. Even toddlers are not getting enough exercise. As with any worrying trend, there are always several (or many) contributing factors; there is never only one cause. But too much screen time is one of the major causes.

- **Moving makes children strong.**
  The less children move, the weaker their muscles become, so after a while active play may even begin to feel physically uncomfortable. That makes sitting in front of a screen all the more appealing.

- **Weakened muscles in the back and core lead to poor posture and also adversely affect gross-motor skills, such as running, hopping, skipping, cycling, catching and throwing a ball and all sports.**
  We can see how a vicious circle can easily develop. When too much time in front of a screen leads to problems with movement activities, the child becomes self-conscious about his poor performance. He retreats even

further into Screen World, avoiding the activities that feel physically or emotionally uncomfortable. Without sufficient practice his muscles will stay relatively weak, and his physical skills are not likely to improve. This reinforces the tendency to avoid those activities and to spend more and more time where he feels most successful, which is in front of a screen.

- **When posture deteriorates due to weakened muscles, internal organs are squashed.**
  Breathing will be more shallow because the lungs don't have room in the compressed ribcage to expand fully. The shallow breathing takes in less oxygen, so less oxygen reaches the brain, resulting in fuzzy thinking, poor problem-solving, even a distaste for thinking. This mild oxygen-deprivation also contributes to learned helplessness, which is the assumption that a task or activity will be too difficult, even before you try.

How too much screen time affects our children's nutrition

- **When a child is in front of a screen, he is literally a sitting target for junk food commercials.**
  These advertisements use sophisticated psychological tricks to excite children's immature brains. The result is a craving which bypasses normal age-appropriate self-control.

- **And even if there is no exposure to these commercials, nutrition can be impacted.**
  When we're absorbed in a screen activity and hunger strikes, we don't feel like taking the time or making

the effort to prepare food. It's so much easier to grab a bag or a box. This is likely to be junk food: high sugar, high salt, high fat – calories devoid of nutrition. We know that junk foods and refined carbohydrates are not good for our children's bodies, but you may not be aware that these foods also influence our children's moods, contributing to grumpiness and over-reactivity.

- **Screens are very absorbing, which leads to mindless eating, not noticing the internal signals of fullness.**
  Studies show that when people of all ages are in front of a screen they consume more than they realise. This is true not only of passive screen viewing but also of interactive use.

How too much screen time affects our children's behaviour and brain function

- **The official figures from the Office of National Statistics are worrying.**
  Children who are on screens for four or more hours a day have lower levels of well-being than children who are on screens for one hour or less a day.

- **Screen use affects the brain rather like a drug, sapping motivation to do anything other than stay in front of a screen.**
  Scientists have found that passive screen viewing changes brain wave patterns within the first thirty seconds, shifting from predominantly beta waves (alert

and attentive) to alpha waves (unfocused and receptive). Reading, on the other hand, keeps the beta waves active.

Once you're plugged in to Screen World, doing anything else feels like too much trouble. Adults who use screens to 'relax' in the evenings know this only too well. Even going upstairs to bed when you're tired feels like too much of an effort.

Using the computer for learning

When parents buy their child or teen her first computer, the expectation is that she will use it for homework and school projects, as well as for fun, and that it will help her learn. Parents and teachers hope that computers will motivate children to want to learn, that computers will lead to self-directed learning, that educational games will provide necessary repetition in an interesting format.

However, when researchers measure the educational impact of children's and teens' screen use, they find that the more time children and teenagers spend in front of a screen, the more their test scores decline. Mathematics, reading comprehension and essay-writing are all affected. The only skills that computer use definitely improves are computer skills, but we know that children and teens are so motivated to use computers that they will learn all the necessary digital skills anyway.

Academic achievement requires critical thinking, attention to detail and the willingness to persevere with a challenge. Computers encourage the opposite kinds of information processing. Computer use reinforces a short attention span and a quick reaction time. Plus, of course, the more time kids spend playing games on computers, the less time they are spending on homework, reading, revising and school projects.

Screen images change very quickly, often several images per second, and when people use computers they click onto new pages very quickly. This activates and reinforces the parts of the brain that govern impulsivity, anxiety and aggression. To make the most of their education, our young people need to be involved in more activities that use and reinforce the parts of the brain that govern planning, prioritising, anticipating, organisation, sequencing, self-control, critical thinking, understanding cause and effect and understanding motives. They will get this through conversation with interested adults, through reading and through real-life experiences. But computer use expands to fill free time so there is less time available for conversing with adults, less time available for reading, less time available for real life and less time available for education.

- **Many of the things that are good for our children require them to make the effort to concentrate on something they don't much feel like doing: homework, revision, reading, music practice, household chores.**

  Many parents have noticed that the more time children and teens are allowed to spend on screens, the less cooperative and motivated they are and the less willing they are to concentrate on doing their best at any activity or task. Too much screen time puts children in a grumpy, argumentative, disrespectful mood. One mother told me:

'A while ago we got back in charge, and screen time became one hour a day instead of three hours. Quite quickly we had our nice, polite boy back again.'

- **The fast-paced nature of interactive computer games, with images that change every few seconds, leads children to expect instant and constant distraction.**

- **There is anecdotal evidence that too much screen time also tends to make children less confident about trying unfamiliar experiences, less willing to take healthy risks.**
  The more time children spend on a screen, the more likely they are to assume that a new skill will be difficult to master, and the less comfortable they will feel making a sustained effort to master a new skill. This reinforces the preference for screen time as the primary leisure activity. Another result seems to be that children become more susceptible to peer pressure. They are desperate to fit in, and that becomes more important than summoning up the courage to follow their own interests in the face of possible teasing or derision.

Electromagnetic radiation
This may sound like a term from science fiction, but there is growing evidence that radiation from electronic devices is harmful to our bodies and brains. In the UK and the US, not much attention has been paid to this, but in recent years several countries have passed laws that aim to protect children from the potentially harmful effects of this type of radiation.

How too much screen time affects toddlers and young children

Toddlers and young children are notorious for having a very variable attention span. They can focus for a surprisingly long time on activities they choose for themselves. But they have a very short attention span for activities not of their own choosing, such as paying attention to instructions. They are very easily distracted. As children grow and mature, their attention span naturally improves. But too much screen time seems to slow down or even derail this natural trend towards more efficient concentration.

- **A recent study revealed that the number of hours a two-and-a-half-year-old spends watching television correlates with how likely he or she is to be bullied at the age of twelve.**
  One reason for this is that more time in front of a screen leaves less time for family interactions and for playing with friends. It's through real-life relationships that children learn how to stand up for themselves.

- **Statistics tell us that for each additional hour a week that a toddler or young child spends on a screen, the more likely he is to be diagnosed with AD(H)D a few years later.**
  There are a number of possible contributing factors. One is that screen activity seems to activate impulsivity, reactivity and novelty-seeking, all of which are characteristics of AD(H)D.

How too much screen time affects children's social skills

The views of Baroness Susan Greenfield, professor of pharmacology at Oxford University, are considered extreme and controversial by some. She is outspoken in her belief that as screen time replaces human contact, children are suffering from less well-developed social skills and from problems regulating their emotions. In her latest book, *Mind Change* (Rider, 2014) she suggests that too much screen time can result in difficulties with learning to delay gratification and with a lack of empathy, as well as a shorter attention span.

Based on my professional observations, Greenfield's point of view is not at all extreme. Every day I hear from worried parents who complain that as a result of spending hours a day immersed in Screen World, their children and teens are actually losing the social skills and the social confidence they once had. This generation of children are not as good at expressing themselves, verbally or in writing, as we would expect them to be given their age, their native intelligence and their education. They are not getting enough practice.

Eye-contact is a form of body language that is necessary for positive social interactions. Eye-contact is a natural behaviour, like smiling or walking, that does not need to be taught. But it does need to be modelled in order for it to become a habit. When a screen absorbs a lot of a child's leisure time, he is receiving less eye-contact from family and friends so he gives less eye-contact.

There is no substitute for plenty of relaxed, stimulating, face-to-face communication. During these interactions children learn how to empathise, how to apologise, how to suggest tweaks to an activity, how to go along with suggestions made by others, how to make someone laugh, how to refrain from doing things that annoy others. It's through face-to-face experiences that children develop the habits of sharing, of waiting their turn, of winning without gloating and losing without blaming or tipping over the Monopoly board. All these skills add up to knowing how to communicate, how to make and keep friends.

How too much screen time affects children's language skills

From infancy through adolescence, our children acquire most of their facility with language through back-and-forth conversations. This is how new vocabulary enters their spoken and written word bank. This is how they learn to understand more complex sentence construction. This is true even of voracious readers; it's easy to assume that their advanced comprehension and their excellent spoken and written language are the result of their many hours of exposure to the printed word. But research tells us that even children and teens who read a lot for pleasure learn a great deal from discussing what they have read. Reading by itself is often not enough to improve communication.

Listening is not enough because it is too passive. If a child is not expected to reciprocate, there is no reason for her brain to pay careful attention. So most of the words she is supposed to be listening to and absorbing and thinking about simply wash over her. This is what happens at school when teachers talk <u>at</u> pupils. This is what happens at home when parents don't require a sensible response. And this is what happens when a child or young person is in front of a screen. Words are going into the ears, but the brain is not really switched on to listening, understanding and remembering because no response is required.

Screen time: The 'mood dummy'

The more time children spend in Screen World, the more they want to dive into it to relax and to calm themselves when they are upset:

> 'My son is five years old. He's sensitive and gets upset about little things. When he can't have the toy or the dessert or the playdate he has his heart set on, he immediately whinges for the telly. When I let him have it, he's calm in a minute. You can see why I give in.'

And when children get more screen time than is good for their bodies, brains and moods, they can easily become hooked; they can become indiscriminate screen consumers. If they're not allowed their favourite screen activity, they'll settle for almost anything else that's screen-based, even programmes or games that are quite babyish for them or that ordinarily they wouldn't be interested in. One mother reported:

> 'Back in the bad old days, before I got back in charge, my kids managed to get hours and hours of screen time on most days, even though I was against it. One day I lost my temper, and on the spur of the moment I banned all TV and computers for the rest of the day. Jamie, who was 13, sulked for about five minutes. Then he perked up and dug out an old video camera and sat there watching videos of himself

practising his skateboarding tricks from a few years ago. He couldn't stand not being on a screen.'

One father I spoke with called his daughter's mini-tablet her 'mood dummy'. A mother complained that her son's phone was 'chewing gum for his eyes'. With screen time as a comforter, children don't learn how to self-soothe when they are upset.

When a child is tired or annoyed about something or in an irritable mood, parents may suggest television or a video to help him relax or calm down. One mother of a highly strung ten-year-old boy told me, *'Television suits my son. He comes home from school angry most days, and TV helps him cool off.'* This is short-term thinking. Some things feel good in the short term but not in the long term. Screen time does often work in the short term to distract a child and change his mood, but meanwhile he isn't learning anything about how to manage his emotions or how to think clearly about what he really needs.

Instead of taking the easy way out, I recommend that if you can spare the time, you stay with him for a while, either playing or chatting or doing chores together. If you can't do this, require him to do something that's not in front of a screen for half an hour or so. Over time this will help you to wean him off using electronics to manage his mood.

In-app purchases

Designers of children's computer games and apps know how to make them very appealing, even addictive. Children sometimes discover that it is possible to use the same password for multiple purchases. Some huge debts have been racked up in this way. Sometimes the child is aware of what he is doing, but often he is not. Young children are particularly susceptible to this temptation when they're playing online games that encourage them to collect jewels or 'treasures'. These games keep children quiet and occupied so it's easy for parents to focus on getting things done, losing track of what children up to. Stay in charge by making sure to turn off in-app purchases.

CHAPTER 5
TEENS AND PRETEENS

Now I want to talk about the effect on preteens and teens of <u>what</u> they are doing in front of a screen, both the content and the type of screen activity. We can't afford to be ignorant of what life is like for modern teens.

Social media

Social media has a lot to answer for. Certainly in small doses it is harmless fun. But due to the addictive nature of screens, small doses, when unchecked, often become large doses. This is true even for adults, who, in theory at least, have more mature self-control. Social media promotes the phenomenon of FOMO, which is an acronym for 'fear of missing out'. This is a big part of the reason why young people are glued to their phones. The compelling ring tones, the buzzing and beeping and vibrating make the message that is coming in seem more urgent than what is happening around them right now and more important than the person in front of them. This fear of not being part of what's happening with one's friends and acquaintances often leads to 'over-sharing' and then to feeling a loss of privacy.

For too many teens, there is no clear separation between online and offline; a young person can come to feel that he is the sum of the experiences he posts or tweets about. Instead of focusing on interactions with the people nearby (usually family or friends), teens check in with social media to see who wants to interact with them, who is interested in them. They are being reactive rather than proactive.

Sarah, aged 17, explained:

> 'I feel hurt if I see pictures of a party I wasn't invited to. The other day I was at a party and having a good time. But the next day I felt bad because no one there thought I was popular enough or pretty enough to post a picture of me. I know it's stupid to feel upset, but I can't help it.'

On social media people of all ages tend to make themselves and their lives look better than they really are. Teens compare their own quite ordinary lives and experiences to this unreal picture of perfection, and they understandably feel inadequate. This phenomenon has earned Facebook the nickname 'Farcebook'.

Social media can also change the way our teens behave offline. Humans evolved as 'pack animals' and as such, we feel the need to be accepted by our pack or group (however we may define that group – family, friends, colleagues, classmates, our profession, our religion, the team we support, etc). To be accepted into a group we need to fit in; our attitudes and behaviour need to be similar in some important ways to the attitudes and behaviour of others in the group. For this reason, we are all very influenced by the beliefs and preferences of the people we spend the most time with. We tend to copy their habits, often without realising that we're doing it. This is true of adults, and it's even more true of children and adolescents, who haven't yet lived long enough to forge a strong identity.

Social media multiplies the number of people in a young person's group and exposes him to many influences that parents are often unaware of. Behaviour that is dangerous (like anorexia) or morally wrong (like bullying) or against the law (like stealing) can start to seem like normal behaviour within a group. This leads to a form of mob mentality, where common sense and empathy and knowledge of what's right and what's wrong are swept aside by the urge to conform. School refusal, physical aggression, underage drinking, eating disorders, inappropriate sexual activity, gambling, stealing, doing drugs, self-harm – these have all become 'copycat' behaviours amongst certain online groups that endorse and glamourise these activities.

In the past decade there has been a huge increase in 'cutting' and other forms of self-harm, particularly amongst teenage girls. I've heard girls talk about cutting in a very matter-of-fact way: how many times they've done it, who amongst their peers cuts and who doesn't, which girls' parents know about it and which don't, who's going to a psychiatrist, etc. Shockingly, suicide is often talked about in the same way, as if it's just another option, a normal, OK solution that a young person might choose.

Of course we can't blame social media alone for these societal ills. When young people are so troubled that they feel the need to resort to physical or emotional self-harm, we can assume that there are multiple factors contributing to their unhappiness. The part that social media plays in this worrying trend is that it normalises this destructive behaviour. This makes is so much easier for young people to bypass their self-control, which is likely to be immature and fragile in the first place.

Cyber bullying

Cyber bullying is any form of bullying that takes place via electronics. Surveys reveal that most young people in the UK have experienced being bullied at some point, either face-to-face or online. But for some, it becomes a fact of life, something they feel they have to live with. In the old days, if you were bullied at school, at least home was a safe haven, but that's no longer the case. The bullying follows you home, and it can be relentless; because of mobile phones and social media there is no escape. In extreme cases, cyber bullying has led to school refusal, depression, anxiety disorders, self-harm and even suicide.

Often a child or teen won't confide in his parents about the bullying because he feels embarrassed or ashamed. He may believe it's his own fault that this is happening to him; he may think that he should know how to put a stop to it. Over time he may come to believe the nasty, hurtful things that are being posted about him.

The teen may worry that he'll be told to close his Instagram account, which he doesn't want to do. Or he may assume that parents will say some version of, *'Just ignore them, and when they see it's not bothering you, they'll stop'*. This may be true, but it's the rare young person who has the confidence and self-discipline to follow that advice.

There are many excellent websites that offer very useful advice about cyber bullying. Some of these websites are aimed at parents, some at young people. In addition to learning how to stay safe on the internet, you and your children can learn how to report bullying or abuse on various social media, how to remove or block contacts, how to close an account, how to delete offensive comments, even how to make a complaint to the police.

When your eyes are opened to this side of young people's screen use, you will probably be horrified to learn how many different forms of cyber bullying currently exist. And new forms pop up regularly as technology becomes more sophisticated.

However, as useful as the information on these websites is,

it doesn't address certain very relevant issues. Most of these websites don't mention the fact that the more time children and young people spend on a screen, the more likely they are to become either victims or perpetrators of cyber bullying. This is another very good reason for limiting screen time.

Every book, website or article on the subject lists low self-esteem as a consequence of cyber bullying, but low self-esteem is often a precursor as well. Children who don't feel good about themselves are often the ones who are singled out as victims. What is less well understood is that emotional vulnerability also leads young people to become bullies. By improving the self-esteem of our children and teens, we can help them to become emotionally stronger and more robust, more asser-tive, more willing to share their problems with a trustworthy adult. Every strategy in Section Three of this book will help strengthen your child's self-belief. This is not a guarantee that nothing bad will happen to him in Screen World. But strong self-esteem will make a difference.

Multi-screening

There is evidence that the habit of 'multi-screening' (attempting to pay attention to two or more screens at the same time) has harmful effects.

Linda Blair, a clinical psychologist, is worried about this trend. She was quoted in the *Guardian* newspaper on 1 April 2015:

'The effect, at least in my clinical experience, is to make the viewer more distractible, less able to concentrate, focus on and later remember what was happening at the time, and less able to make decisions. This, in turn, has a negative impact on schoolwork and self-confidence.'

Violent and other inappropriate screen content

Many preteens and teens are exposed to films and television programmes intended for adults, and they play online games that are not appropriate for their age. This is happening when children are home alone, but also when the parents are home but pre-occupied with their own concerns. Or parents may be watching this content while the children are around, seemingly oblivious. Preteens and teens are exposed to inappropriate themes, images and words, not only extremes of violence and irresponsible sexuality but also more subtle but unhelpful and unrealistic stereotypes of gender, race, socio-economic status and beliefs.

Children have sponge-like memories so it would be naïve of us to assume that they're not being influenced by what they hear and see. Many studies have shown that aggressive images, language and themes on screen lead to aggressive thoughts, words, beliefs and actions, especially with boys. In their interactions with siblings, parents and peers, these children are copying what they have seen and heard, often without quite realising they are doing anything hurtful or anti-social.

Violent computer games are even more influential because they are interactive. As the child's character is killing, maiming, blowing up or destroying, he is visualising himself doing those things. This normalises aggression as a legitimate reaction, as a solution, as a fun pastime.

On-screen violence, whether passive or active, often leads to anxiety, especially amongst children who have a more extreme temperament and are already prone to anxiety. Such a child may react to disturbing images or story lines by developing unreasonable fears, for example of parents dying unexpectedly or of his home being destroyed by a tsunami or earthquake. This child may feel like he is being bullied (when adults can see only normal joking and leg-pulling), or he may be so convinced there are monsters lurking behind his bedroom door that he won't go upstairs by himself.

Over the years, many parents have shared with me their worries about how anxious their child seems to be. In every instance, the anxieties and phobic reactions were significantly reduced within a few weeks of parents getting back in charge in two important ways: eliminating most of the upsetting content on screens and also reducing the total amount of screen exposure.

Pornography

Children and teens have always been fascinated by sexual images, without any harmful effects. But the type of pornography that is prevalent on the internet does have harmful effects. An article in the *Guardian* newspaper on 1 April 2015 quotes the results of a survey: ten percent of twelve and thirteen year olds are worried that they might be addicted to pornography.

And now there's also 'revenge porn', in which sexual images are forwarded, posted or 'shared' on social media sites without the consent of the original sender and with the purpose of causing embarrassment or distress.

Unless closely supervised, children and teens of all ages may stumble onto websites that they don't have the maturity to process adequately. Twenty-first century pornography is very graphic, misogynist and violent.

A recent study revealed that the average teenager spends an hour and a half a week surfing the net specifically looking for pornography. Before the internet, children and teens looked for sexual images and found them; that is nothing new. One of the things that is new is the average age at which children first are exposed to pornography. Before the internet, the average age for boys was eleven; even that statistic may come as a shock to many parents. But in the last ten years that age has become even younger. And what children are seeing are increasingly violent images. Some psychologists have identified teens and preteens actually suffering from post-traumatic shock from some of the violent pornographic images and videos they have seen.

Of course young people are curious about sex, so of course they will use the internet to find out about sex. Often they are not deliberately looking for pornography; they may be looking for information or even for reassurance that they are normal.

Some people assume that there is no difference between internet pornography and the pornographic magazines that have always been available. There are in fact two very important differences. Teens have always had access to soft porn magazines, but usually not to magazines portraying sadistic, violent sexual images. The internet makes all of that easily accessible.

The other important difference has to do with moving images versus still images. Moving images are much more believable. They are processed in the brain almost as if the person is watching something real that is happening, whereas still images do not have that same impact on the brain. A teenager with a magazine might look at a picture for a while and then turn the page and look at another picture. But our eyes tend to stay glued to a screen. On the internet it is easy to get swept away by the story that is unfolding. Numerous studies conducted in different countries have shown that people who are exposed to a lot of pornography have more difficulties with relationships.

We will need to be proactive and to raise the subject with our children, working on the assumption that most teens and many preteens have been exposed to pornography, whether we are aware of it or not. This is a time to be practising what I call 'outer calm', even though you will probably not be feeling calm on the inside.

Overreacting will convince teens that you are a hopeless fuddy-duddy, not in touch with the realities of the world he lives in. Rules about not searching for pornography won't work. Punishment or threats of punishment will not be effective. Those reactions will shut down communication and convince your teenager that you don't have a clue.

Parents assume that teens would be too embarrassed to talk about sex with parents. It is true that teenagers are easily embarrassed, mostly because they desperately want to believe that they are more grown up than they are. But teens have lots of questions and lots of anxieties about sex, and they are often secretly grateful when the same-gender parent broaches the subject.

Our teens are more likely to trust us if we don't react with shock and horror. Teens are already predisposed to worry that they are weird, that there is something wrong with them. We don't want to unintentionally reinforce that distorted view of themselves.

First you will need to gain your teen's trust so that he is not worrying about whether you will be lecturing him or telling him off. To build trust we need to commit to spending some Special Time every day (see Chapter 18). If you often don't arrive home until after bedtime or if you are out of town a lot, you can still keep up the daily Special Time by phone.

If you are wondering what you could say to get the conversation started, it helps to depersonalise it at first. Rather than asking them about their experiences or their opinions, you could say, *'What do your friends think about sexting?'* or *'I've heard people can get just about anything on their mobiles nowadays.'*

We want to make sure that teenagers understand the difference between realistic sex and fantasy sex. This isn't too difficult to bring up in a general, casual way because we are surrounded by advertisements that depict fantasy sex. We also want our teens to understand the negative effects of pornography, that it teaches nothing about love and affection and respect. In fact, it teaches the very opposite. These are tricky, complex concepts to get across so be prepared to revisit these conversations many times over the growing-up years.

Because many teens turn to the internet for information about sex, you need to be careful which sites you block when you put parental controls on the computer. You want to block the pornography sites, but still leave access to the websites that provide legitimate sex education.

We can expect young people to experiment, even though we might wish they wouldn't. Thankfully, when we help our teens to feel better about themselves and to feel better about the relationships within the family, their experimentation is likely to be short-lived and self-limiting. That's because they will be more influenced by the family's values than by the values of the teen subculture. As a result, they will be less prone to all types of addictive behaviour, including pornography, eating disorders, self-harm, drugs and overdosing on electronics. The strategies that I introduce in Sections Two and Three will help improve children's and teens' self-esteem.

No parents want to believe that their teen might be addicted to pornography. If this seems like a possibility, you need to take it very, very seriously. It can affect self-esteem, peer relationships (with both genders), schoolwork and relationships within the family.

Of course you will need to make sure you don't inadvertently feed the addiction by allowing electronic devices in the bedroom. But that won't be enough. You will also need to examine the family relationships and the messages that your family is giving to the teen, and you will need to get professional help. You can start with your doctor or the school counsellor or a Twelve-Step program. Addiction to pornography is serious.

Racial hatred, anorexia, self-harm and suicide websites and forums

In addition to pornography, there are websites and forums that promote and glamourise racial hatred, anorexia, self-harm and even suicide. It's hard to believe, but these sites do exist. And they can be surprisingly appealing to a young person who is going through a hard time for any reason. It seems to her as if a lot of other young people are going through the same thing, and it's comforting to feel part of a group.

If you even suspect that your child or teen is drawn to these types of topics, consider it a warning sign that he or she is not coping well. The strategies that I talk about in Sections Two and Three will be very useful for helping teens feel better about themselves, but these strategies alone may not be sufficient. When teens are very troubled, professional help is often necessary.

Sexting

Sexting has become a widespread phenomenon, but it didn't exist a generation ago when today's parents were growing up. So parents are worried and confused – with good reason. The definition of sexting is the sending or receiving or posting via any electronic device of sexually suggestive or provocative or explicit photographs, videos or text. Influenced by online pornography, these images and videos have become more and more graphic. If you have a teenager, don't assume that your son or daughter would never be involved in sexting. In fact, receiving a sext can even happen by accident – just click and open. Then what will a teenager do with the image or video or text? Statistics tell us that far too often he or she will forward it to a friend, rather than confiding in a trustworthy adult.

There has been a huge increase in teenage girls being persuaded by their boyfriends to strip in front of a webcam and touch themselves. Willingness to do this is generally related to shaky self-esteem, often combined with revenge against parents. If you suspect that your teen is involved in any form of sexting, you will need to take action immediately. But you will probably need to do more than get rid of the webcam and insist that all electronic devices are kept in the communal areas of the home. You may also need to focus on transforming the parent-child dynamics so that the family becomes the kind of group that the teen wants to belong to. That will allow her to be influenced by your values, rather than rejecting them.

A lot of sexting amongst teens (and increasingly amongst preteens as well) is driven by normal curiosity, by the habit of electronic 'sharing' – and of course by the poor judgement that we can expect from otherwise sensible young people when they are tempted by an exciting and forbidden activity. Girls may send these images so they can boast that someone thinks they're 'hot'. This can make them feel better about themselves because in the teen subculture appearance matters more than character or personality, despite what parents and teachers preach. One result of this trend is that girls feel pressured and manipulated into posing for the camera. They're taunted and labelled prudes if they're not willing to.

In a recent survey, the charity BeatBullying found that more than a third of eleven to eighteen year olds have received a sext. You may be convinced that this sort of thing is not happening in your community. You may be right, but don't be complacent because teen trends like this can spread rapidly. And parents are always shocked when they discover that sexting goes on amongst 'nice' kids who have good exam results and high aspirations, from stable, loving families. One negative effect of sexting is that the image or text may be forwarded to the recipient's friends, either intentionally or accidentally, often causing great embarrassment and shame to the original sender. And young people who send or receive sexts are shocked when they discover that even a deleted photo or text can be retrieved from the innards of a mobile phone or computer.

The laws regarding sexting are complicated and in some cases vague. So police are able to use their discretion about how to handle those cases that come to their attention. It is against the law for a young person under the age of eighteen to send a naked photo of himself or herself. According to newspaper reports, a fifteen-year-old girl who sent her boyfriend a naked picture of herself from her phone was charged with possession and distribution of child pornography, even though she herself was the child in question. Another newspaper article reported that a fourteen-year-old boy had been added to a national police database after he sent a naked picture of himself via Snapchat to a female classmate. She then 'shared' it electronically with her friends. The boy's mother was quoted as saying, *Apparently it happens all the time. It is just how teenagers flirt these days'*. The police file remains active for a minimum of ten years, and it can be accessed by potential employers.

Gambling

Research indicates that online gambling is appealing to younger and younger children. This is partly due to how it is marketed, with pictures of cute animals. Gambling can become a serious addiction because it stimulates the release of certain brain chemicals that make a person feel good. Interestingly, the excitement of not knowing how something will turn out activates this process even more than the experience of winning. So it makes sense to put these games, apps and websites off-limits.

The great teen myths

'Everyone else is allowed to . . .

>*go on their computer before they do their homework.'*
>*text during dinner.'*
>*play 18+ games.'*
>*stay in their room and not come down for dinner.'*
>*keep their phone in their room overnight.'*

And:

>'Everyone else's parents buy them a new computer and pay the tariff on their mobile.'

Once children start secondary school, you may never meet or even talk on the phone with the parents of your children's friends. So it's easy to doubt yourself and start to wonder if maybe it's true that 'everyone else' really is doing all those things. And children are so convincing when they say it! But whether it's true or not is beside the point. Have the courage of your convictions. Don't let yourself be swayed by the intensity of your teenager's screen dependency. This book will show you how to stay positive, firm and consistent.

'It's mine so I'll do what I want'

You may be confused when your child or teen claims that because he bought the device or game or app with his own money or was given it as a present, he should be able to use it whenever he wants:

> *'It's not fair!'*
> *'But it's mine.'*
> *'You have no right to tell me what I can do with my own private property.'*

Once again, remember that you are in charge. Your job is to transmit your values. Whenever possible, pre-empt this problem. Before the new device enters your home, clarify the new rules.

'I'll lose all my friends'

Your preteen or teen will probably complain that he will be left out of social arrangements if he doesn't have access to his mobile at all times. You may be desperate for your child to feel confident or popular so you're tempted to give in, allowing more screen time than you know is good for him. It's easy to believe that any restrictions on screen use would result in your child or teen being teased or excluded for being different, for not being cool. Be strong! Your teen's anxiety won't be lessened by your giving in.

'I need the computer for my homework'

If your child tells you that he needs the computer to do his homework, of course you want to believe him. But you may be dismayed when you walk into the room to see his screen suddenly switch from Facebook or YouTube back to his homework. We want to trust our children, but let's be realistic. If he has attempted to deceive you in the past, he is likely to do it again. Make sure that when he is doing his homework in front of a screen, he is in a public part of the house. And make sure that his back is to you and his screen is facing you so that you can easily see what is happening on his screen.

You may believe (or almost-believe) your child or teen when he says he needs a better, cooler, more expensive device than the one he has. You may feel guilty that you can't afford to give him what he is so desperate to have. However, we know that children who get what they want too easily become spoiled. Be brave and stick to your principles.

Homework: The problem with using computers

It has become very common for children and teens to copy from the internet or to print out text from websites, which they then include in their homework and projects as if it is their own work. It is so easy to do, so quick, so tempting. But this is plagiarism, and it undermines one of the main purposes of homework, which is to give pupils practice at thinking for themselves.

Parents have a right to expect that the school will notice

and take action on plagiarism. Some schools do; some don't. Some teachers do; some don't. Unfortunately, we cannot count on teachers to hold students accountable for doing their best, so it is the parents' job to require children and teens to put everything they learn into their own words. Expect resistance at first:

'But everybody does it.'

'But the teachers don't care.'

'But it would take too long.'

'But it won't sound good if it's in my own words.'

Of course your child is right about the last point. He isn't as fluent and articulate as the adult who wrote the text for the website he's copied. We know that is not the point; we know that the point of the homework assignment or the project is for him to learn something, not just to impress. But don't bother lecturing; it will fall on deaf ears.

We want him to know how to produce work, in his own words, that he can be proud of. You may need to set aside the time to teach your child how to use his own brain and his own words, instead of copying from the internet.

In my earlier book, *Calmer, Easier, Happier Homework*, I walk parents through how to guide children and teens into the habit of doing their own thinking.

Don't lose your nerve when he comes out with all those *'buts'*. Instead of trying to convince him that it won't take too long, be honest: *'Yes, it will probably take you much longer to write it in your own words.'* When children and teens complain that they don't have enough time, what they usually mean is that they would rather be spending time with their friends, in person or via a screen.

But sometimes when they say they don't have the time, they're actually right. For many teens, a combination of

after-school activities, a heavy homework load, maybe
sports or music practice, means that below the surface
they are feeling anxious and overwhelmed a lot of the
time. Sometimes cutting and pasting from the internet is
one of the ways they've discovered to help them cope with
the stress.

The mental health of adolescents is adversely affected
by a lack of unscheduled leisure time. When teens have
fewer commitments and more unstructured, non-screen
free time, they are less stressed, and they become much
more willing to do their best on their homework, rather
than to take shortcuts such as copying from the internet.

Monitoring the content of your teen's screen use

Some parents believe that the content of their teen's online
activity and their virtual relationships should remain private,
that it is none of the parents' business. These parents believe,
or more likely they desperately hope, that they can trust their
teen to be sensible. This approach can work well – until a teen
is tempted or lured, or simply stumbles, into a part of Screen
World that is unsavoury – and finds himself in over his head.

Parents may not feel comfortable with the idea of monitoring their children's screen use, but they may feel that the
potential dangers justify it. Even parents who believe it is their
right to monitor what their children are doing online may draw
the line at using covert means to find out who is texting or
posting what to whom.

Software exists that will enable you to do this if you decide
you need to (see Appendix B). But if the trust between parent

and teen has deteriorated that far, then monitoring screen activities is not likely to be enough to resolve the problem. You will also need to devote time and thought to rebuilding the parent-child relationship.

If you learn how to foster an open dialogue, you will be better able to keep yourself informed about the content of your children's on-screen activities without invading their privacy. The strategies in Section Three will help you to achieve this, but it probably won't be easy.

CHAPTER 6

WHY SCREEN TIME IS SO ADDICTIVE

This may seem like an unnecessary question to ask. It could be that you don't really care why screen time has such a hold on our children – perhaps you just want to know what you can do about it. However, there is a good reason to explore this question. Understanding the causes of a problem often gives us valuable insights into which solutions will be the most effective.

In this chapter I will be exploring several factors that contribute to children's and teen's preoccupation with screens. Some of these factors are historical, some have to do with the home environment, and some have to do with a physical and emotional predisposition.

Physiological reasons

There is a scientific reason for screen cravings, preoccupations and addictions. It is very difficult to ignore screens because thanks to evolution, our eyes are genetically programmed to follow movement. Humans have evolved to monitor our environment by continually scanning it for changes that might signify danger. Most of us no longer live in environments that are physically dangerous, but we still have a strong residual instinct to notice and react to changes in our environment.

You have probably noticed that if you're in a room where there is a screen on in the background, your eyes tend to keep drifting back towards the screen, even if you don't even like what is on the screen. Screens suck us in, even when we're not the slightest bit interested in what's happening on the screen, even if it's in a foreign language and we don't understand a word of what's going on.

Another reason for the mesmerising effect of screens is the speed with which the images change. Our eyes tend to stay glued to the screen because the information is coming at us faster than our eyes and brains can process it.

Children and teens experience a burst of serotonin, the 'feel-good chemical', when they accomplish something online, when they score or win or move up to the next level or when their character kills someone. This good feeling make them want more and more. And with practice they usually get better at the game. As a result, they will win more so they will feel that serotonin rush more often.

Environmental reasons

The environment surrounding our children and teens influences what they do, what they think about, what they care about, what they aspire to.

The environment of a typical modern family predisposes young people to screen dependency. In addition to mobile phones and other hand-held devices, there is frequently a screen in every room, often with the furniture pointing towards it. This sends the subliminal message that being in front of a screen is the norm; in fact, it's one of the main activities that happen in that room.

Many families own so many screens that they have literally lost count. When I do in-home consultations, I often ask each family member to write down, without saying the number aloud, how many screens there are in their home. Typically, no one comes up with the same answer, and no one in the family knows the correct number. Each parent has forgotten about one or more of the devices owned by some other family member.

From a very young age, children see parents scrolling through emails and texts, preoccupied, not answering children's questions properly, barely looking up. Children don't understand that the largest part of the parents' screen use is related to work or to other commitments. Children can't see that this screen activity isn't fun. All they see is how absorbed their parents are in Screen World, and understandably they are intrigued.

The examples we set for our children and teens are very powerful. Our children naturally absorb the habits and values of their environment, So if we are in the habit of 'switching off' and 'relaxing' in front of a screen of an evening, is it any wonder that our children will sooner or later come to believe that this is what they too need to do to relax?

Young children usually have a variety of activities they enjoy, both outdoors and indoors. Sadly, as they approach the teen years, many of these pastimes and interests fall away. This is partly due to peer pressure, the drive to fit in and to seem cool. Partly it's due to the creeping presence of electronics. And partly it's a result of not seeing parents and other adults in their world enjoying a variety of activities.

Siblings are another very influential part of the home environment. Younger siblings usually look up to older siblings and want to copy them. So they tend to watch the same programmes and films, play the same online games and visit the same social media websites, many of which are unsuitable for their age group.

And of course the environment outside our home is also saturated with screens: public transport, waiting rooms, restaurants, schools, adverts on the street.

Evolutionary reasons

In primitive times life was dangerous, and humans learned that there was safety in numbers. So we evolved with a strong drive to be part of a group. As our brains evolved beyond instinct, we learned most of what we needed to know to survive by imitating others in our group. For our survival, evolution saw to it that we felt comfortable and safe and normal when we were accepted as part of a group that was similar to ourselves. To be accepted into a group, a person needs to fit in, needs to like and care about and think about what the other members of the group like and care about and think about.

For most of us, life is no longer a matter of survival, but evolution has not caught up yet. Most of us still feel more comfortable when we have the acceptance and approval of a group of people we can identify with, even if it's a virtual group.

As adults, we have the life experience to be discerning, to choose wisely which groups we want to identify ourselves with. But young people have not lived long enough to develop this wisdom. They are likely to want to be part of whatever group seems to be the most exciting – or the most accepting. And once they feel part of a group, they will be very influenced by the norms of that group.

Since time immemorial until a few generations ago, the influential group that children and adolescents and young adults wanted to be accepted into was the extended family and the surrounding community of families with similar values and habits. Children and young people modelled their actions and beliefs on those of their elders, and this led to acceptance within the group, to approval, appreciation, trust, loyalty and a sense of pride.

For a number of reasons, in the past hundred years or so, these stable communities began to breakdown and disperse.

Into the vacuum rushed a different kind of group altogether, a group made up of peers. The influence of trusted elders waned. Children were influencing children, and teenagers were influencing teenagers. It may be hard to imagine that the concept of teenagers as a separate group or community with its own values and its own tastes in clothes and music hardly existed before World War II. This trend has continued and intensified.

If you look back in history you will see that there have always been groups of teenagers and young people who set themselves apart from their elders. But until relatively recently, these groups tended to be young people from the upper classes, with too much time on their hands, too much money for their own good and not enough that was expected of them. In the twentieth century, this phenomenon spread to all socioeconomic groups.

Freud gave us the idea that it is normal and even necessary for young people to go through a stage of emotional development during which they rebel against the values of the community they grew up in. He called the process 'individuation'. But most of the time young people at this stage are not really focused on exploring their individuality. Rather, they seem to be switching their allegiance and their drive to conform from their family to a community of their peers. But this concept of individuation can be comforting and reassuring for exasperated parents. It can be invoked to excuse or legitimise teens' rudeness, disorganisation and lack of motivation.

Freud saw something that was happening in affluent, urban areas, and he assumed it was universal. In fact, in parts of the world where young people still have real responsibilities within the family and within their community, this rebellion is rare. Instead, as young people grow up, they become _more_ respectful of their elders and _more_ motivated to show what they are capable of.

You may be familiar with the concept of youth or teen 'subcultures'. These are groups of young people with distinct styles, behaviours and interests. A lot of scholarly research has gone into identifying these subcultures and seeing how they are similar to and different from one another. There are scores of teen subcultures at any given time, each slightly or very different from the others. But most of these groups have a few things in common. One is disdain for the adults in their lives. Another is a dependency on electronics; screen activity is the currency of inclusion. Many teens, and nowadays many children as young as nine or ten years old, think of themselves as belonging to one of these groups.

One huge problem with children and teens defining themselves by their peer group is that they are being influenced by people who are at the same level of experience and maturity – or rather at the same level of inexperience and immaturity.

If we want our children to grow in experience, maturity and wisdom, we can't ignore the influence of the group they feel accepted by. We need to remember how important it is for our children to feel that they are valued members of a group. We need to give them a better group to want to belong to. For the sake of our children's well-being, now and in their future, we can, and I believe we should, reinstate the family as the group that our children and teens want to align themselves with, the group they feel allegiance to. Once we understand and accept our children's and teens' need to be part of a defined group, we can consciously decide to remake our families into the kinds of groups that our children want to belong to and want to identify themselves with.

Of course, we also want our children to feel comfortable and confident navigating the wider world outside the home. But we don't want them to be too influenced by the least sensible and least mature aspects of that wider world, so we need to give them a firm foundation of values, skills and habits.

We can do this in a number of ways. We can make our home a place where children and teens feel good about themselves because they feel appreciated and understood. We can set a good example, exposing our children and teens to a wide range of potentially interesting and fulfilling activities. We can involve our children frequently in activities that will expand their horizons. We can foster their strength of character. We can do everything in our power to limit the harmful effects of the outside world, including Screen World, until our children have the maturity to make wise decisions. The rest of this book explains how the Calmer, Easier, Happier Parenting approach can help you to achieve these aims.

Emotional reasons

There are several important emotional reasons why screens have such a hold on children and young people. Children, and especially teenagers, often feel criticised and blamed by parents and teachers. Screens, on the other hand, are completely non-judgemental, non-critical. In Screen World there are no parents telling them off, no reminders, no exasperated looks, no lectures, no threats. Also, because young people are usually better than their parents at everything to do with screens, adults are effectively excluded from a large part of their children's lives.

Many teens and preteens are over-scheduled with homework and extracurricular activities. Not having enough guilt-free downtime causes stress. Young people frequently turn to electronics when they are angry or anxious. They know from past experience that time in front of the screen will help them relax temporarily by taking their mind off their worries. For many, Screen World is a haven of calm.

Nowadays even young children are showing signs of emotional stress, and many children as young as five years old report worries about body image, exams, money and divorce. Screens are a comforting escape from the real world, a welcome distraction.

Other activities gradually lose their appeal; they seem boring or they feel like too much trouble, compared to on-tap entertainment. So screen time becomes the preferred pastime, which leads to further loss of interest in non-screen activities. Cause and effect turn into a vicious circle. We can't expect young people to know how to get themselves out of this trap, or even to want to. That's our job, and we <u>can</u> do it.

CHAPTER 7

WHY DOES GETTING BACK IN CHARGE FEEL SO DIFFICULT?

This chapter explores in depth why parents don't feel comfortable or confident about getting back in charge of the family's screen time. As I mentioned earlier, almost every problem has multiple causes. That's why even seemingly simple problems can be so tricky to resolve. To achieve significant improvement with most problems you will probably need to make changes to a number of contributing factors.

I've identified four main categories of reasons why parents find it so difficult to be in charge of electronics. When parents aren't being true to their values about screen time, probably one or more of these factors are contributing to the inconsistency.

A Parents may not realise the potentially harmful effects of screen time

Often parents do not realise the causal link between the four issues of screen time (see Chapter 2) and problems with character traits such as resilience, respect, responsibility, appreciation, motivation, confidence, cooperation, self-reliance, consideration and doing one's best.

Parents also may not realise the potentially negative impact of electronics on the daily flashpoints: getting up in the morning, mealtimes, homework, sibling interactions, peer relationships, bedtimes, etc.

Parents may justify a screen-saturated home by citing the many beneficial uses of technology:

> *'Schools teach IT, even in primary school. The classrooms have interactive whiteboards and tablets for the children to play educational games. So how can technology be so bad?'*

> *'My son isn't great at literacy or numeracy, but he's so creative. He makes very clever videos on his phone. He wants to do that when he grows up. I don't want to deprive him of that.'*

These are valid points. But let's remember that screen time can be constructive or harmful, depending on how the four issues I mentioned earlier are handled: how much screen time your children and teens are having, what they are doing on the screen, when and where.

If things start to go wrong with homework, revision, music practice or household chores, parents may assume that their child or teen is simply not motivated to do his best. They may view their child as 'lazy', not realising that the quantity and quality of screen time is a major contributing factor.

B Parents may have some mistaken beliefs about their children and technology

Parents understand that children and teens need to relax and unwind between school and homework, and they assume that screen time is the best or only way to relax:

'After a long day at school, my kids are tired and fed up. They need some unscheduled time to just flop, to switch off and do whatever they feel like.'

Children and teens definitely do need some unscheduled time to call their own every day. However, there are several problems with the habit of relaxing in front of a screen after school. One is that screen activity isn't refreshing and restorative, compared to real-life activities such as playing, creating, moving their bodies, reading or listening to music. Time in front of a screen is enjoyable while one is doing it, but it often leaves people more irritable and impatient. Screen time right after school is likely to make homework, revision, music practice and household responsibilities even less appealing than they already are. So let's not allow our children to drift into the habit of turning to Screen World when they want to relax.

Parents may believe that children and teens can do a good job on their homework and revision and household chores while part of their attention is on a screen.
It's a myth that multitasking is an effective way to get things done. The facts are:

- Pupils who often multitask get poorer exam results.
- When people are multitasking, they take longer to complete their tasks, and they make more mistakes than if they concentrated on one task at a time.
- People remember less of what they learn when their attention is divided.
- Even when both tasks are simple, multitasking impairs performance.
- A significant amount of time is lost in switching attention back and forth between tasks.

- People who regularly multitask end up with poorer concentration even when they are doing only one thing at a time.
- Multitasking causes a temporary drop in information-processing ability, the equivalent of about ten IQ points. This is the same result as if you went without sleep for a full night.
- Habitual multitaskers don't realise all of the above, and they typically believe they are more effective than they really are.

Parents may worry that putting limits on screen time might keep children from becoming proficient in computer skills. One parent said:

> *'I want to give my children every advantage. And technology is the future.'*

We never need to worry about whether our children will master the digital skills they will need in order to be able to function in the modern world. They are very motivated to learn, and the learning is fun for them. They learn quickly and easily because they are confident, and success breeds success. You and your children can embrace all that is good about technology. Just make sure that your values prevail when it comes to how much screen time they have, what they are doing on the screen, when and where.

Parents may think that 'I'm bored' is a problem.
Boredom is not a problem. Boredom just means there is no stimulation coming in from the outside, and the child hasn't decided what he feels like doing next. If the option of being entertained by a screen or a parent or a playdate is usually available, children lose confidence in their ability to create their own entertainment. Children need lots of unscheduled,

screen-free time in which to feel 'bored' so that they have to fall back on their own resources.

Parents may believe that their child's temperament would make getting back in charge terribly stressful or maybe even impossible.

If a child has always been whingey and demanding, parents may believe that he could not learn to entertain himself without screens. If the parents assume that a child is so stubborn that he would rather do without screen time than 'give in' and follow the new rules, then the parents won't be motivated to follow through. As many parents can attest, even strong-willed or inflexible children can be guided into more sensible habits if you use strategies that are very positive, very firm and very consistent.

Parents need to change too
Parents may feel it would be hypocritical to restrict a child's screen time when they themselves are often on their phones and computers. Similarly, if parents have a television or computer in their bedroom, they may secretly agree when the child complains that it's not fair that she can't have an electronic device in her bedroom. The solution here is for parents to be willing to change their own habits in order to set a better example.

C Parents may be confused or discouraged and no longer trust that they know how to get back in charge of screens

Many parents have tried in the past to establish sensible screen time rules and routines, but it hasn't worked as well as they had hoped. Now they don't trust themselves; they no longer have the confidence that they can get back in charge of the family's screen habits. Here are some examples:

Parents may no longer be clear about the ethics of imposing their views on their child.
They may not be sure that they really have the right to make rules, to influence habits, to transmit their values. They may worry that attempts to establish new screen habits would be 'dictatorial' or 'controlling', trampling on their child's rights.

Naturally we want our children to feel good most of the time and to enjoy their lives most of the time. The problem comes when a parent believes that children need what they want. This is another ways of saying that children can't be happy unless they get what they want. If you believe this, you won't feel comfortable putting limits on screen time; it will feel as if you are being cruel.

Parents may feel defeated by their child's angry, stubborn reaction to the new screen rules and routines.
Parents may blame themselves, their partner, the child, the peer group, the times we live in. But actually there is no need for blame at all. Things went wrong because the parents weren't equipped with the right tools for the job.

We know that practical tasks require tools. Without the right tools, it's hard to open a tin can, hammer in a nail, sweep a floor. In the same vein, you'll have a hard time reducing screen dependency and establishing sensible habits unless you have the tools that are suited to the job. That's what this book provides – a set of tools or strategies that will help you get back in charge.

Often parents do know how get back in charge. The

problem may simply have been that they were using strategies that would have been effective if they had carried on, but
they expected to see results quite quickly so they gave up too
soon. If they had persevered, the very stubborn child would
have become less stubborn. Another possibility is that the
parents used effective strategies sometimes, but weren't
consistent. That can make a stubborn child even more
stubborn.

Parents' feelings can be very hurt by the awful things children and teens can say when the supply of their 'drug' is
threatened:

'Get a life.'
'I'll go live with Dad.'
'You can't make me.'
'You just read that in some stupid parenting book.'
'You're a control freak.'

Parents feel so frustrated when their child doesn't take the
new rules seriously:

'I'll just do it when you're at work.'
'Dad lets us.'

When we are in the grip of a strong emotion, often we can't
think very clearly. When parents are angry and desperate,
they may issue an ultimatum or threaten a sanction that they
can't or won't follow through with.

You may have experienced how easy it is to declare an
extreme consequence as a knee-jerk reaction when you lose
your temper. You may say, *'No screens for the rest of the week.
And if I hear one more word out of you, that'll be another week
of computer gone!'* In your moment of fury it may feel good to

vent, but quite soon the guilt sets in; you realise the consequence you threatened was over the top. So you apologise or
you conveniently 'forget' about the consequence after a few
days. Or you tell the children they've 'earned back' their
screen time by being extra good. Each time something like
this happens your children will lose a bit more respect for
you.

Parents may be discouraged and perplexed because they
would never have dared to disobey or argue back to their
parents the way their children do. The parents are flummoxed;
they just don't know how to insist effectively when their child
or teen refuses or threatens them.

**A parent may be feeling very stressed for a variety of
reasons.**
The main causes of stress for the modern parent seem to
be: working too many hours, not spending enough time
doing things he or she enjoys, not spending enough time
with family and friends. Whatever the reason, stress takes
its toll on us. We have difficulty staying positive and being
consistent. Stress can actually rob us of the ability to think
clearly. And you do need to be thinking clearly in order to
get back in charge of the technology in your home and to
stay in charge.

**It may not really be a matter of getting back in charge
of electronics. Possibly the parents never felt confident
that they could be firm about screen time rules.**
Electronics may be just the tip of the iceberg. It may be that
parents never got the hang of requiring cooperation about the
other daily flashpoints either. This is most likely to happen
when you have a child with an extreme temperament or when
you have several children very close in age, which can feel very

stressful and overwhelming. Sometimes parents don't know how to insist on cooperation. Parents tell me:

'But he's bigger than me.'
'I can't physically make him do what I say.'
'Children are different nowadays.'

The good news is that we can always guide children and teens into the twin habits of cooperation and self-reliance, regardless of how big they are. Being in charge is not about size. Even when children are very small, it's not possible to physically make them do anything (although you can physically stop them from doing things, which is not the same thing).

You've heard the old saying, *'You can lead a horse to water, but you can't make him drink'.* There's a second part to this saying that you don't hear very often: *'You can make it much more likely that the horse will drink by salting his oats.'* Let's 'salt the oats' by focusing on guiding, motivating and influencing, which is very effective at any age, if you use the right tools. Sections Two and Three will give you some helpful tips for guiding children and teens into the habit of cooperating the first time you ask. In addition, I recommend that you read the first book in the Calmer, Easier, Happier series: *Calmer, Easier, Happier Parenting.*

A separated or divorced parent may find getting back in charge even harder.
A separated or divorced parent may feel very discouraged if she (it usually is the mother) is the 'stricter' parent. That usually means she has more rules and clearer rules and follows through more consistently. A separated or divorced father is likely to be more lenient or indulgent about screens for several

reasons. He usually spends less time with his children so he doesn't want their time together to be marred by uncomfortable, angry interactions. He may also want to do whatever he can to be liked by his children. And he may want to prove that he is different from the other parent.

Or he may park the children in front of a screen because he is not confident that he knows how to play with them or chat with them; he's lost touch with what his children like to do and like to talk about. He may give in to pleas for more screen time because he feels guilty that he can't spend more time with his children. He might even feel guilty that he doesn't want to play with them. And lastly, he may believe that a parent's job is to entertain, to keep the cries of '*I'm bored*' at bay.

D Sometimes it suits parents to allow more screen time than they know is good for their children and teens

Parents often use screens as a way to get some peace and quiet:

- So that parents can sleep in at the weekend
- So that children won't misbehave in restaurants or in the car
- So that a parent won't be interrupted when he or she is trying to concentrate on a task, such as making dinner, or on work
- So that parents can have an adult conversation without being interrupted
- So that a restless or impulsive child won't pester the parent with demands:
    'I'm bored.'
    'I'm hungry.'
    'Can I . . . . . .?'
    'Will you . . . . . .?'

> *'I need . . . . . .'*
> *'I want . . . . . .'*

- So children won't get into things and either make a mess or do something dangerous
- So that a child will stay sitting at the dinner table.

It's tempting to use screens as pacifiers, but it's short-term thinking because children won't be learning sensible habits. Many children behave much better at school or at a neighbour's house than they do at home. This proves that they know how to be cooperative and self-reliant, but they are in the habit of behaving differently in different places. We can guide our children into the habit of behaving more sensibly at home. That way you won't even be tempted to use screens to try and manage their behaviour.

By switching on a screen, parents can instantly eliminate a lot of sibling unpleasantness.
However, as soon as the screen goes off, the siblings will be back where they started because no teaching or training has taken place. The siblings are not learning how to resolve or manage conflicts. If you would like your children to get on better but you're not sure how to teach and train more sensible habits, let me direct you to two of my earlier books, *Calmer, Easier, Happier Parenting* and *Calmer, Easier, Happier Boys*. Each of these books has a chapter that focuses on how parents can help improve sibling relationships.

When we're in a hurry because the schedule is too tight, we want to be left alone to get things done as quickly as possible.
Screens to the rescue! Let's commit to building a cushion of time into our daily routines so that we're not in such a rush.

That way we can include our children in many of our tasks, rather than putting them in front of a screen so that we can get things done.

Conclusion

In this section I have laid the groundwork to help explain why it's so important for you to get back in charge of the electronics in your home. In the remainder of the book I will show you how.

HOW TO GET BACK IN CHARGE OF THE ELECTRONICS IN YOUR HOME

CHAPTER 8
HOW TO LIMIT SCREEN TIME

Different families choose to limit electronics in different ways. In fact, one way might work well for a few years, and then as the children enter a different stage you might want to shift to another way. You can adapt any of the methods I suggest here to suit your family, and you can even combine several.

Remember that you're in charge. Don't try to persuade or encourage your children to limit their screen time; no matter how well-intentioned you are, your words will feel to your child like lecturing and nagging. Remember that being in charge is about you making the important decisions, staying true to your values.

Limiting screen time is about moderation; it's not all or nothing. It's like sweets: too little and children feel deprived, but too much and they won't feel good or behave well.

Don't expect things to go smoothly at first. Your children will make mistakes, and so will you. They will test you to see if you mean what you say. How you handle rule-breaking and rule-bending, whether occasional or habitual, impulsive or deliberate, will determine how quickly your children get used to this new way of life. The strategies in Section Three will help you to reduce misbehaviour.

If your child or teen is very fixated on screens, take several small steps to reach your goal, rather than expecting that she can do it in one big leap. Here's how one family put this advice into practice:

'It seemed like my daughter was always on her phone. One day I added it all up, and it was almost six hours! My husband and I decided we'd be fine with two hours a day, but we knew she'd need to get used to it gradually. So we did it in stages, first telling her four hours a day and then about a month later it went down to two hours. She minded of course, but doing it gradually made it easier for her – and for us! By the way, she's a different person now. She's taken up the guitar again, her marks are much better, and she's so much nicer to be with.

First, decide on screen-free days and screen-free times of day

One popular way to start loosening the addictive hold of electronics is to have whole days when no screens are allowed at all
Here are some possibilities:

- No screens at all Monday through Thursday.
- No screens at all Monday through Friday.
- Screens allowed only on odd-numbered days of the month.
- No screens on one or two days each week, usually on days that are packed with after-school activities.
- No screens during half-terms.
- No screens for one week of each school holiday.
- No screens for the whole of the summer holidays.

The above list can feel very scary for parents. *'How will the children react? How will they entertain themselves? How will I keep them from squabbling?'* Every parent who has been brave enough to embrace whole days without any screens, whether it's one day a week or several weeks at a time, has found it to be enormously beneficial. Children rediscover sports, hobbies, reading, nature, board games and hanging out with parents.

Having screen-free days every week works very well for families with children who don't yet have their own mobiles. If you feel that it may not work so well for your older children, Chapter 9 will explain how some screen time can be earned as a reward every day – a very motivating concept for preteens and teens.

Work towards my guidelines of no screens for under-threes, half an hour for ages three to eight, and one hour for ages eight upwards

This means that even on days when children can have some screen time, there need to be times of the day that are screen-free. Routines reduce resistance, so we can harness the power of routines to achieve this. We will need to have a daily routine so that everyone knows when certain things are happening:

- I've explained how screen time changes mood and brain function, undermining motivation to concentrate on anything other than a screen. So a really useful rule is no screens before school, before homework and revision and before music practice.
- Set aside a certain time of the afternoon or evening for homework, with no leisure screen use allowed during that time, not even during the breaks between subjects.
- If the rule is '*No screens at all during dinner*', that means no one can even peek at an incoming text. This rule results in a screen-free half an hour or so.
- It's a good idea if after dinner, instead of immediately scattering, the whole family pitches in to clear the table,

do the washing up, clean the kitchen, feed the pets, empty the bins, etc. If you have a rule that no screens are allowed during this family chore time, then this is another fifteen or twenty minutes that is completely free of screens.

- If you start a routine of spending twenty minutes or so each evening hanging out with each of your children individually (see Chapter 18), that is another chunk of time with no screens.
- We can establish Family Time (see Chapter 18) in the evening between homework and bedtime. Once again – real fun, not screen fun.

Second, prepare your environment to limit screen time

There are many actions parents can take that will change the home culture so that it is no longer dominated by screens. We want the home to be an environment that is about people relating to each other face-to-face and doing real things together. We can prepare the environment to make it easier for all family members to shift their focus away from screens and onto real life. Here's how:

Establish a drop-zone near the entrance to your house or flat.
Every family member, parents included, deposits all their mobiles, tablets, laptops and other devices here on the way in. The norm becomes not being in front of a screen. You can decide how often and when family members will have access to their devices.

Put passwords on every single device.
And don't let your children see you tapping in the password.
Be willing to log in or out every time. It may be inconvenient,
but it's worth it for the peace of mind.

Remove all the remotes when not in use.

**Don't buy any more screens and get rid of the ones you
no longer need.**
Remove the duplicates, the broken ones, the older models that
got stuffed into a cupboard and forgotten when the new, more
exciting model came along.

Keep televisions and computers out of bedrooms.

**Set up an overnight charging station that is near where
you are in the evenings, not near the children's bedrooms.**

**If you hide any devices to keep them off-limits, be
thorough; hide them where they really won't be found.**
If you lock them away, make sure you keep the key with you. In
the first few weeks of limiting, when children and teens may
be feeling acute withdrawal pains, many parents take the
handheld gadgets and spare laptops with them to work or lock
them in the boot of the car. One mother told me what her tech-
savvy son managed to do:

> 'He was on his tablet hours and hours every day. Finally I had had
> enough. I found what I thought was a very clever hiding place for
> it. He promptly used another device to locate the hidden one – he
> somehow made it beep! I had no idea that was possible. Now I
> keep his tablet under lock and key until he's allowed to have it.'

Use all of the mechanical and electronic means at your disposal to limit screen use or to disable certain functions.

We can install software programmes that block the internet after a certain time in the evening. We can block certain sites. We can arrange to see our children's search history. Put a timer on all the devices your children and teens use.

Yes, some kids are very talented at hacking into parental controls. Even if you're sure that will happen, still set the controls. Your children will see that you are serious about the limits you've made rules about. You'll still have to be vigilant, though.

Set screen limits for the adults as well, so that every day you can point out to your children when you are abiding by those limits.

Don't take advantage of a few minutes of peace and quiet to scroll through your work emails. Save that for a specific time, and make sure your children know when that time is.

When you're taking care of a commitment via a screen, whether work or personal, announce what you're doing so your children don't think you're having fun:

> *'I'm paying the electricity bill.'*
> *'I'm confirming that we're going to the Hendersons next week.'*
> *'I'm filling in the form for your class trip.'*
> *'I'm looking for a good dog kennel for Scamp while we're on holiday.'*

Because many children find almost everything to do with electronics fascinating, they will often respond by wandering over to take a look at your screen. This gives you a perfect opportunity to teach many important life skills. And your children will gradually discover a whole other side of electronics that isn't just about fun.

Once you've decided when screen time can happen, post those times where everyone can easily refer to them.
Then when children ask if they can turn on the television or play on the tablet, just point to the chart. Smile while you're pointing so you won't seem annoyed. Soon they won't be asking; they will have the chart memorised.

You may be willing to believe that you could be in charge of your home's electronic environment if you have a preteen and maybe even a young teen. But you may worry that you could not possibly make the limits stick with an older teenager. You can. Regardless of his age, regardless of how tall he is, regardless of how good he is at arguing, our job as parents is still to teach and train, to transmit the values, skills and habits that are important to us.

Why just setting a time limit often doesn't work
If you've been in the habit of setting a time limit for screens, but then getting absorbed in what you're doing and losing track of the time, your child will be on the screen for longer than the stated time before you notice. If this happens a lot, pretty soon she will stop taking your time limit seriously. And she's likely to be more annoyed when you finally insist that she has to switch off.

Of course you'll need to stay alert so that you can see if your children are staying within the limits you set. But you won't need to police the four screen issues forever. As your children get used to the limits, they will be developing more mature habits. You'll find that you can gradually give them more responsibility for self-monitoring.

Third, decide (with your partner if you have one) how you will introduce the new plan to limit screen time

You and your partner will need to get united on two levels. You will need to both agree, by compromising if necessary, to the principle of limiting screen time. Next you need to agree on the fine print, the specifics of exactly how much, what, where and when.

After you and your partner have taken the time to sit down together to clarify these points, you will feel much more confident that you can persevere and insist. Of course the rules and routines you come up with together will be a work in progress. No matter how carefully you think things through in advance, there are bound to be some little wrinkles that didn't occur to you when you were planning, or some unusual circumstances that pop up unexpectedly. You will have to revise and tweak your rules and routines as you discover these, but when you first introduce the screen time limits plan you need to feel that you're starting out on solid ground. Taking all the time you need to plan will help you feel less defensive or apologetic. You will be able to explain the plan clearly and simply and calmly.

Becoming a United Front

It often happens that electronics feels like a big problem to one parent but not to the other parent. This is more likely to happen if one parent has quite an easy-going temperament while the other is more highly strung and easily upset. It can also happen when one parent has a tendency to focus on the big picture, not noticing or remembering which rules have been bent or broken, whereas the other parent has sharp attention to details.

Generally parents share core values and have similar goals for their children. But often parents have very different ideas about how these goals should be achieved. That's because 'Opposites attract'. Different temperaments and personalities lead to different parenting styles. In fact, at our Centre we have noticed, time and time again, that *'Opposites attract – at first. But once you have children, opposites annoy each other'*.

So you and your partner may have very different ways of approaching parenting issues, including the four issues of electronics. You may be sure you're right and your partner is wrong. If only your partner would see it your way, that would solve the problem!

When parents don't agree on what the rules surrounding electronics should be, these are some common complaints. One parent says:

'What happens is my wife and I make a rule about what the children have to do to earn their screen time, and it's OK for a while. But pretty soon she forgets about the rule, and then I see the kids on their gadgets with the beds not made, home- work not done, a mess everywhere.'

'My husband works in television so his whole life is about screens. Even at home. He'd rather be looking at a screen than playing with the children.'

'When I go out for few hours at the weekend, when I come back, the whole family is in front of one screen or another. My husband can't be bothered to do something constructive or interesting with them.'

The other parent counters with:

> *'What's the big deal about a little extra TV at the weekend? Why can't we relax the rules once in a while?'*

> *'Sometimes it feels like my wife is running the house like the army. I'm a more spontaneous kind of person. If my children want to watch something at the "wrong" time, I say let them. You can imagine the rows this causes.'*

> *'I have a very stressful job, and the last thing I want to hear when I get home is crying and whingeing. I say let them watch. It calms them down.'*

Somehow it always seems to be the fault of the other parent! Family life can be very stressful if you don't have a United Front. Unresolved problems allow resentments to build up and fester. Even with the best will in the world, each parent is likely to start blaming the other. The resentments may be minor, and you may be able to forget about them for stretches of time, until something happens to trigger the resentment. Unresolved problems are rather like a tiny pebble in your shoe. At first you hardly notice it; then it feels uncomfortable but not bad enough to take the time to do anything about it; then eventually it feels so uncomfortable that it's all you can think about.

Thankfully, it is possible for parents with very different temperaments or personalities or points of view to become united in their parenting policies and rules. To become united, each parent will need to compromise. Compromise never means that one parent has to give in and do it the way the other parent wants. That type of 'solution' always breaks down sooner or later. The parent who has given in eventually becomes resentful. Plus, the parent who gives in will probably not be motivated to stick to a plan that he or she doesn't really like. That parent may forget to follow through with the plan, or he may forget the details of the plan. When that happens, the other parent is understandably upset. After all, the partner agreed to the plan (or so it seemed at the time), and now he's not taking it seriously.

It doesn't have to be this way. Rather than trying to get your partner to agree with you, you both need to accept that you each have a right to your perception of the situation, no matter how misguided it seems to the other parent. Only then can you hope to reach a compromise. My definition of compromising is that both parents get enough of what they want so that they feel satisfied, but they give up some of what they want so that the other person also feels satisfied.

We often avoid facing what's not working well in our family because it all feels hopelessly complicated; everything impacts everything else so you don't know where to begin. Maybe you can only think of a solution for part of the problem, or maybe the only solution you can come up with would cause other problems. Or maybe you can think of a really good solution, but it feels like too much of an effort, especially if you dread how your children, or possibly even your partner, will react when you broach your idea for a solution. Maybe you're worried your partner will blame you for causing the problem. Maybe you're blaming yourself. Maybe you're worried it will turn into a huge row, or you'll be left with a tense, uncomfortable atmosphere. So you shy away from opening that can of worms.

But I hope I have shown you that clearing up the smallish problems before they grow into bigger problems will help the couple relationship and the parent-child relationship to be calmer, easier and happier. And even if the screen problems you're grappling with are no longer smallish, you can still find solutions.

Resolving problems with a *solution talk*

It really is possible to reduce resentments by learning to compromise. So how does a couple become united on an issue when they really don't see eye to eye? The *solution talk* is the strategy for forging a realistic compromise. The *solution talk* is the antidote to all those reasons you have for not talking about a problem with your partner. With the *solution talk* strategy neither you nor your partner will be focusing on the problem, which usually just leads to arguments and hurt feelings. You'll be focusing on solutions.

A *solution talk* is a strategy for arriving at a compromise without falling into the traps of complaining or blaming. A *solution talk* has rules and a specific format; it isn't an ordinary conversation or discussion.

Here's how to do a *solution talk*

Parents set aside fifteen minutes, no more and no less. Set a timer so that you don't have to keep checking the time.

There need to be no distractions:
- Make sure all screens are off.
- Don't start the *solution talk* when either parent is hungry.
- Don't start the *solution talk* after nine-thirty p.m. When you're tired, it's easier to be irritated and to start complaining, and it's harder to stay focused on the positive.

- Don't do the *solution talk* where your children might be able to overhear you. If you're worrying about that, you won't be able to focus your full attention on the process.

Alternate which parent starts first.
Take turns choosing the issue to tackle.

The parent who starts will say one sentence, and one sentence only, about an issue that is troubling or annoying them.
This could be a big issue or a very small one.

If allowed to, you and your partner could wax eloquent about the problem because you know it so well. You could explore every nuance of the problem; you could probe into every little nook and cranny of the problem. If you allowed yourself to do that, it could easily use up most of the allotted fifteen minutes. And talking at length about problems usually just makes us more upset, which makes it harder to think constructively about solutions. And the more you talk about a problem, the more likely you are to blame someone – either your partner, your child, yourself or 'society'. Even if you're not blaming, your partner may feel blamed and may become defensive, which then makes it difficult to listen to each other and to think positively.

Here are some real-life examples of how parents summarised their issue in one sentence:

'Let's talk about how we can get Jamie to finish his revising before he goes on the iPad.'

'I don't want the children watching TV while they're having their tea anymore.'

'We need to do something about the kids' bickering over who can use the computer and when.'

'I caught Harry with his mobile under the covers last night.'

Each of you will take it in turn to offer a solution, again in only one sentence.

You both write down all the suggestions, yours and your partner's, exactly the way the sentence was said, using exactly the same words.
That way there is no room for misinterpretation.

If you don't like any part of the solution your partner just suggested, you are not allowed to say so.
Instead, you have to make a counter-offer. Here's an example:

Father: *'Let's take the phones away at bedtime.'*
Mother: *'Instead of us taking them physically, let's have the children put them in our room to charge at night. That way they'll be learning self-reliance.'*

Keep alternating coming up with possible solutions until together you reach a compromise you can both accept or until the fifteen minutes is up.
Usually, parents reach an agreement about what to do about a problem even before the fifteen minutes is up. Occasionally the timer goes ding and you haven't come up with a solution that both parents are willing to put into place. The next day simply carry on from where you got to the day before. You both have verbatim notes of who said what so it will be easy to pick up where you left off.

Do a *solution talk* every single day until you have no more problems or issues left to sort out.

That day will never dawn, of course, so do a *solution talk* every day. It only takes fifteen minutes so it's always possible to squeeze it in, even on a busy day. If you and your partner aren't in the same location, you can do a *solution talk* by telephone or Skype or FaceTime so there's never any excuse for skipping a day. Soon you will have a calmer, easier, happier household.

CHAPTER 9
SCREEN TIME AS A REWARD

In many families, children are getting more screen time than the parents think is good for them, although it's probably less than the children want. Every once in a while, when parents are at their wits' end with frustration about clothes left in a heap on the floor or homework being turned in late or curfews being broken or chores being neglected yet again, parents will threaten to take away the device or ban it for a while.

Sometimes parents do actually follow through with their threats, although on average a consequence is threatened four times before a parent finally takes action. During those first three threats your child's respect for you is dwindling because you're not following through; you don't seem to mean what you say.

When parents do eventually follow through with the consequence of curtailing screen time, the child may be very resentful because it was not set up in advance that the screen time was conditional on certain behaviour. The screen time was just a fact, something she had a right to, with no strings attached. When you take something away from a child that you have allowed her to have, it feels very unfair and it breeds resentment. There is a better way: **earning screen time as a reward**.

Earning is completely different. Earning is about doing something in order to get a reward. With earning there is no entitlement to screen time. Instead, screen time is the reward children can earn for following the parents' rules.

Why is using screen time as a reward better than taking it away when things go wrong?

There are several important benefits of requiring children and teens to earn their electronics (as opposed to letting them have it in the usual way and then taking it away, or threatening to, when they misbehave).

Because screen time is so motivating, children and teens will do almost anything you ask in order to earn it. If your child knows that he has to make his bed and be gentler with his little brother and do his piano practice without complaining, he'll be doing all those things and more, probably within a few days.

More and more parents are choosing to have some screen-free days every week. This works very well for families with children who don't yet have their own mobiles. But for teens and preteens, especially if you are having difficulty motivating them to improve some habits (doing his best on homework, chewing with her mouth closed, being flexible when playing with a sibling, hanging up her bath towel, doing what she's told the first time, etc.), then the chance to earn a daily reward of some screen time can be very helpful.

By taking the time to put a consistent reward system into place, you will be able to guide your child into sensible habits without repeating, reminding, nagging, lecturing and blaming. Very soon family life will be calmer, easier and happier.

With repetition, children and teens soon get into the habit of doing whatever they have to do to earn their screen time, even behaviours that they previously resisted or that were outside their comfort zone, for example stroking the new baby instead of squeezing, sitting down to start homework at the right time, remembering to say please and thank you, coming off the computer without a fuss, keeping their bedroom tidy, being brave about taking a guess when they're not sure if their answer is correct, etc.

Quite quickly these actions become easier and easier to do. After a while these new positive habits become automatic and even enjoyable. This may seem too good to be true. Yes, we really can motivate our children and teens to get into better habits by using rewards.

How long will this take?

It partly depends of course on how consistent you're willing to be with the rules about earning screen time and with all the strategies I talk about in this book. It also depends on your child's innate temperament. With a child who is by nature more sensitive, intense, impulsive, inflexible or immature, it usually takes longer to establish new habits. This is true even if the child is very bright. He may be advanced in some areas, but when it comes to new habits, he may be a slow learner. Do persevere – it will happen!

So much of life, both as a child and as an adult, is about deferring gratification, doing something that in this moment we may not feel like doing in order to get something we want in the future. As our children are earning rewards, they are learning first-hand about accountability, a concept and a life skill that will help them to be successful at whatever they undertake, now and in the future.

Any mood-altering substance or activity, including screen time, changes the user's brain chemistry, creating strong cravings; the brain wants more and more. This craving or obsession comes from the most primitive part of our brain, the part that is concerned with survival. To the addict it feels as if he

<u>must</u> have his fix – or he will die. And sadly, that's how screen dependency can feel to a child or teen. She <u>must</u> have it. She can't imagine herself or her world without it – and she has to have it right now! That's why children will plead, whinge, pester, argue, insult, lie, scream, sneak, take the iPad without asking, or even become physically aggressive to get a bit more screen time.

But something fascinating happens as soon as screen time has to be earned. Suddenly the thoughts surrounding this mood-altering activity are processed in a completely different part of the brain, the pre-frontal cortex. This is the newest part of the brain to evolve, and it is the seat of thoughts that distinguish humans from our closest animal relatives. The pre-frontal cortex is what makes us civilised and rational. It governs, among other things, organisation, planning, sequencing, and an understanding of cause and effect. This is often known as executive function.

By now thousands of parents have told me that within days of introducing a reward system for screen time, their children become much less desperate and obsessed by electronics. By the end of the first month of this new plan, their children were almost unrecognisable.

In fact, a number of parents have got back to me a few months after starting the earning plan, complaining that their children no longer cared that much about screen time so it wasn't an effective motivator any more. This is a very good problem to have!

Useful definitions

To clear up any confusion, let me explain what I mean by certain words. A <u>right</u> or an <u>entitlement</u> is something that does not have to be earned. Our children have a right to food, clothing, shelter, affection, education, medical attention, time to play, etc. Children do not have a right to screen time.

A treat is something extra, often unexpected; it too does not need to be earned. Ice cream at the zoo is a treat.

According to the *Concise Oxford English Dictionary*, a reward is something given in recognition of service, effort or achievement. A reward has to be earned.

Because of the hold that Screen World has on children, it's quite likely that when you first introduce your plan for earning screen time, your children, understandably, will attempt to derail you. One typical ploy, which too often succeeds in embroiling parents in an argument, is to accuse the parents of trying to bribe.

The *Concise Oxford English Dictionary* says that to bribe means *'to dishonestly persuade someone to act in one's favour by a payment or other inducement'*. So children are using the word 'bribe' incorrectly on two counts when they use it in relation to having to earn their screen time. First, there is nothing dishonest about a reward system. Second, the purpose of the reward is not to get children to do something for the parents; it's to get them to do something that is good for the children – although undoubtedly you will benefit as well.

Honestly, who's in charge?

The person who is in charge is the person who makes the rules. That's you. You already make lots of rules for your children, and you insist on them. In most families children have to go to school (or be educated at home), they have to do their homework and clean their teeth and say please and thank you and put away their toys. Children may not want to do these things, and they may moan and complain, hoping to get you to change your mind, but they generally don't question your right to be in charge, to decide on the rules. You have just as much right to be in charge of the electronics in your home.

When parents first hear about the earning strategy, they may feel that a reward system is similar to the way animals are trained. Parents may believe that because humans are rational beings, capable of reasoning, we should try to influence our children by reasoning, explaining, discussing, coming to a civilised agreement. If this approach to limiting screen time is working well in your family, you're probably not reading this book! Reasoning with children about screen time is rarely effective because our reasons for wanting them to develop more sensible screen habits are grown-up reasons. Children are not interested in our reasons; they are focused on trying to get what they want. And because screens are physically and emotionally addictive, children will feel like they <u>need</u> their screen time.

When parents try to reason with a child, they often end up repeating and explaining and re-explaining, which feels to the child like he's been told off. And when you try to use reasoning to persuade, you're abdicating your natural authority. As parents we're not perfect, and we don't know everything, but we're definitely more experienced, more mature and wiser than our offspring. Therefore it's our responsibility to transmit our values, and we can achieve this when we have the right tools.

You already know how to be in charge. Now it's time to get back in charge of screen time. Even though you're the one who decides on the rules and routines, of course you'll want to pay some attention to your children's preferences. You want your children to know that you care about how they feel. And by giving children some choice, you'll get fewer arguments so family life will be calmer, easier and happier for all of you. I recommend that you allow your children to suggest small tweaks to the earning plan, but the plan is yours. You are the decider.

It's important that we keep showing our children that we want them to earn their screen time. One father told me:

'I used to say, "If you don't tidy your room this weekend, there'll be no computer for all of next week". I didn't think about how negative and unfriendly that sounded. After going on Noël's course, now I say, "First do this, then you can have a half hour on your tablet". I also say exactly what they have to do, instead of being vague.'

Arrange it so that what your child has to do to earn his screen time is easy enough that on most days with some effort he will earn most of it. But don't set the bar so low that he always earns the full amount. If what he has to do is too easy, it won't feel to him as if he's earning his electronics. It will feel to him like a given, something he's entitled to. Let's keep our standards realistically high, expecting from our children what they are capable of.

CHAPTER 10
HOW TO DECIDE ON A SCREEN TIME REWARD PLAN FOR YOUR FAMILY

At this point you may be wondering how to turn the theory of screen time as a reward into a workable plan for your family. Here's how to begin:

1. The first step is to choose a time when you won't be distracted.
2. Sit down with your partner, if you have one. If you're a single parent, enlist the help of a friend who shares your values.
3. Make a short list of four or five really annoying habits that you want your child or teen to improve. This step is usually easy!

If you are like many of the parents I work with, on your list you may have:

- **Do what you're asked to do the first time you're asked**
  I refer to this as <u>cooperation</u>. Most children and teens do what they're told for six hours a day at school. This proves they can do it at home. Cooperating at school doesn't usually feel like a hardship as long as the teachers are friendly, and it won't feel like a hardship at home either, as long as you stay friendly.

- **Speak respectfully**
  This is a more positive way to say: don't argue, whinge, pester, scream, swear, mutter under your breath, roll your eyes, insult, be physically aggressive, etc.

- **Be friendly to siblings**
  Don't tease, mock, insult, trip up, grab, hurt, etc.

- **Do your homework, music practice and household chores promptly, carefully and thoroughly**

Maybe ten or twenty rules sprung immediately to mind, and you're wishing you could include them all on your list. There's no need to have a long list because most of the things we want our children to do are already covered by the first rule on the list, which is *'Do what you're told'*. Some examples of things we typically tell children to do are household chores, sitting down to do their homework, holding your hand crossing the street, coming off the computer without an argument, telling the truth, cleaning their teeth, helping clear the table after a meal, playing a board game with the family. We don't need a separate rule for each of these.

Of all the habits you've listed, cooperation is the first one that children need to master. Only once they are in the habit of doing what they're told the first time, will they become self-reliant enough to follow the other rules on your list without needing to be told each time.

Start by making a rule that your children can earn their screen time by doing what they're told the first time they're told. Cooperation doesn't come naturally; it's a habit that children have to learn. And rewards make this habit easier to learn.

If your child were suddenly expected to cooperate the first time and without a fuss all day long in order to earn his screen time, he would probably never earn it. But we can teach and train our children to cooperate the first time without a fuss for longer and longer stretches of time. Children and teens will internalise this important habit more quickly and more easily if you start using the strategies I talk about in Section Three. Over time, cooperation will become a habit.

Screen time reward plans

There are several earning plans that have proven popular with the families who consult me. Each has its pros and cons so you can choose whichever one you think would work best for your family.

Here's the screen time reward plan that I recommend for children from about four years old and upwards.

Divide each day into four quarters:

- From waking-up time until school drop-off (at weekends and during the holidays it would be from waking-up time until lunch time)
- From when your child comes home from school until tea or dinner (at weekends and during the holidays it would be from lunch time)
- From tea or dinner until the official lights-out time
- From lights-out time until waking-up time the next morning

Complete cooperation in each quarter of the day will earn your child a bit of screen time, which he can use whenever you decide screen time should be.

Complete cooperation means that your child or teen does what you ask the first time you ask, every single time you ask, for the whole of that quarter.

Let's say that you (and your partner if you have one) have decided on a maximum of one hour of screen time per day that can be earned. With this system of dividing each day into quarters, your child can earn fifteen minutes of screen time for complete cooperation in the morning quarter, another fifteen minutes for complete cooperation in the afternoon, another fifteen minutes for complete cooperation in the evening and another fifteen minutes for complete cooperation between lights-out time and waking-up time.

If your child is below the age of eight and you've decided that he can earn a total of half an hour of electronics per day, then complete cooperation in each quarter of the day will be worth about eight minutes.

The last quarter of the day happens after bedtime so complete cooperation from lights-out to waking-up time counts towards the next day's screen time. This means that most of the time children will wake up having already earned fifteen minutes of screen time, which is very motivating.

On any day that your child earns her screen time in all four quarters of the day, she can have an extra reward. This could be a bit more screen time or some other reward.

You will need to make the time and headspace to check that whatever you ask your child to do is done by a certain time. Otherwise even a child who is usually very honest will be tempted to lie and say she made her bed or finished her home-work when she didn't.

Is some misbehaviour so bad that it should wipe out all screen time for the whole day?

Parents have asked me whether physical aggression should be handled separately from the four quarters. They have suggested, for example, that hitting should result in no screen time for the rest of the day or maybe even the next day as well. I do not recommend that because it's very demotivating. Most hitting, kicking and pushing is the product of impulsivity coupled with anger or anxiety. To guide an impulsive child into more sensible reactions (which can only happen over time, not instantly), it's very helpful if several times a day (the four quarters) he is starting with a clean slate and has another chance to earn a bit of screen time.

Physical aggression can be reduced very successfully with *think-throughs* (see Chapter 15), *action replays* (see Chapter 17) and by committing to some lifestyle changes. By this I mean making sure that your child has optimum nutrition and is getting enough sleep and plenty of exercise every day.

One huge advantage of this quarters earning plan is that you won't be so tempted to ignore an instance of minor non-cooperation; you'll know that even if she didn't earn her screen time for this quarter of the day, she has more chances later in the day to earn some screen time.

When you begin this plan, self-reliance (telling himself what to do) will probably not yet be a habit. You won't be able to rely on your child to remember the household rules from one day to the next (or sometimes even from one hour to the next). So be willing, at the start of each quarter, to make sure your child knows what you expect of him in that quarter. A better way than simply telling him, which often goes in one ear and out the other, is to do *think-throughs*, which I explain in Chapter 15.

Only when your child is cooperating the first time about ninety percent of the time does it make sense to start requiring her to remember to follow the routines without having just been told (self-reliance).

A good way to motivate children to become more self-reliant sooner is to **give an extra five minutes of screen time for each chore they do or rule they follow without having to be told**. In order to be eligible for this extra screen time, a child needs to be on track for earning his reward during the quarter. Otherwise, a child who hasn't cooperated the first time and therefore didn't earn this quarter's electronics might assume that he could do lots of chores to claw back some of the screen time he didn't earn.

An earning plan for a very young or immature child

The quarters earning plan would not work for a very young or immature or impulsive child. His cooperation wouldn't last long enough for him to earn his reward. For this child you need to be willing, at first, to reward a very short period of good behaviour, maybe even just ten or twenty minutes of complete cooperation. For that he might earn five minutes of electronics.

You wouldn't want to do that all day long because he could potentially end up with too much screen time for his age. So target the most problematic issues, which might be getting dressed, cleaning teeth, tidying away toys, staying at the dinner table, saying hello to his teacher, whatever he regularly finds difficult. A timer is very handy. The child can earn a bit of screen time by finishing what you ask him to do, without a fuss of course, before the timer goes ding.

If your child is extremely immature, he might even need to get his little bit of screen time very soon after he's earned it, rather than having to wait until evening. He might not be motivated by a reward that will happen later in the day; it doesn't seem real to him.

A screen time reward plan for a child or teen who is ready to move from cooperation to self-reliance

You can move onto this next method once your child or teen has mastered the habit of cooperation, by which I mean that on most days she is earning all her screen time for complete cooperation in all four quarters of the day.

This new plan will help her develop the habit of self-reliance, telling herself what to do, rather than waiting to be told. Go back to your list of four or five habits that you want your child or teen to improve. Feel free to customise the list of rules to fit your family's needs, but <u>don't have more than four or five rules</u>. Otherwise the list can feel oppressive to your children, and you will have difficulty remembering all the items on a long list.

<u>Phrase your rules in the positive</u> so that your child is hearing about what she <u>should</u> do. She already knows all about what she shouldn't do; she's probably heard a lot about that already. But hearing about what she's done wrong won't motivate her to improve. In fact, it may do the opposite. It may convince her that she is someone who does things wrong a lot of the time. This, as you can imagine, feels very discouraging.

For each habit, make a rule that she needs to remember to do it right for the whole day, without being reminded (for example, to speak respectfully) in order to earn fifteen minutes of screen time. This is harder in one way than the quarters system because she has to speak respectfully all day to be able to earn some screen time for this habit. But it's easier in another way because she can earn her fifteen minutes for one of the habits even if she doesn't earn fifteen minutes for another one of the habits.

On any day that she earns all four of her fifteen-minute rewards she can have an extra reward. This is very motivating. The extra reward could be a bit more screen time, or it could be something completely different, such as getting to stay up fifteen minutes later than her usual bedtime or getting to choose part of the menu for the next night's dinner, etc.

Take your time

Part of this preparation stage is taking the time to decide exactly what your child has to do to earn his reward and also exactly how much screen time he can earn, when he can have it, where, with whom, etc. Don't rush this stage. As you mull it over in your mind, new tweaks and issues will occur to you. Make sure your rules are very clear and very specific and written down before you present them to your child. This is how one couple achieved clarity:

'We were dreading telling our kids the new reward plan. We were worried our teens would find some loopholes they could wriggle through or they would ask us nit-picky questions that we wouldn't have answers for. So we delayed telling them about the new plan for a week. In the meantime we emailed our list of rules and rewards to five of our closest friends. We asked them to see if they could spot any

fuzziness or inconsistencies. And they did. So we tightened up the rules, made them really clear. We went into that first meeting with our kids much more confident because we knew we had a watertight plan.'

Even with careful planning, you won't be able to predict all the little things that might go awry. Each time something new comes up that you hadn't thought of, decide how you will tackle it and build it into your plan.

Family chores time

I strongly recommend that children be expected to contribute to the smooth running of the household on a daily basis. This habit leads to competence and confidence. Rather than you doling out the chores for your children, you can let them choose from a running list of short jobs. I recommend that the whole family spend about twenty minutes each evening right after tea or dinner doing chores. That way you're on hand to supervise, to teach and train, to Descriptively Praise (see Chapter 13) and to Reflectively Listen (see Chapter 16). Your children and teens will be motivated to participate and do their best if that's what they have to do to earn their screen time. Over weeks and months, willingness and more mature attention to detail will become habits.

Making your expectations crystal clear

Because screens are so addictive, children and teens will do whatever they can to wangle a bit more. So we need to make the rules governing how screen time can be earned absolutely clear.

For example, if you are using screen time as a motivator to influence a resistant child or teen to cooperate about revising, you may well need to specify all these details:

- how much revision needs to be done to earn the reward
- starting at what time
- ending at what time
- where in the home the revising will take place
- how many breaks he can take, and when and where, and what will they consist of (not in front of a screen)
- which subjects will be revised
- what method of revising will your child use
- with what type of help and from whom
- with what type of supervision

Giving clear instructions or making clear rules about all the different aspects of revising may seem a tedious chore, but this is the best way to guide a resistant or reluctant or rebellious young person into more sensible habits. Of course we would like to believe that we can take for granted some of these elements of revising without having to spell out all of our expectations. A good motto in this sort of situation is: better safe than sorry. It never hurts to over-prepare, whereas under-preparing can lead to parent and child both becoming upset. The way to Prepare for Success is with one-minute *think-throughs* at neutral times (see Chapter 15). Don't be put off by groans, eye-rolling or *'I know what I have to do; I'm not stupid'*.

Another way to manage a reward system is with points or ticks or stars, which can be 'cashed in' for minutes of screen time (or for other rewards)

You can have a chart listing four or five behaviours, and your job is to notice, throughout the day, when your child has done one of those things right and to give a point or tick for it. Before you begin, establish a limit to the number of points that can be earned so that your child doesn't end up with too much screen time.

The point system is easy to use because you have something concrete to look at and fill in. Keep the chart near where you all have your meals so that you will remember to look at it and to show how pleased you are. Your Descriptive Praise (see Chapter 13) is as motivating as the points are.

Here's another way parents have used screen rewards to improve habits. Children or teens can earn half an hour of screen time for each hour of reading or revision they do.

Of course you'll need to check that the reading or revision was done properly. Otherwise there's too much scope for lying or convenient forgetting.

Other screen-related rewards

The rewards I've talked about so far involve time that can be spent in front of a screen. In addition to earning screen time, here are some other rewards that have to do with electronics.

Rather than you being the one who pays for your child's monthly mobile phone minutes, his quarters of complete cooperation or his daily self-reliance could earn him the money to pay the tariff.

He could earn money for buying games, apps, gems, etc. To eliminate arguments, keep a record (posted on the wall so it won't mysteriously disappear) of money earned and money spent. If you don't trust your child to be completely honest, make sure you are the one who fills in the record. In case you're worried you would forget to record this information, link it to a daily event such as dinner or screen time or a bedtime chat. To make this motivating, don't let your child use his own money to buy these games. He has to earn them by cooperation or self-reliance. And of course, make sure that only the parents know the password or code so that he can't buy more than he has earned.

What rewards can a child earn on a non-screen day?

You will probably find screen time rewards so useful for guiding children into better habits that you may feel at a loss for an effective reward on screen-free days. There are two ways to approach this. You could roll over the minutes of screen time your child has earned to the next day or to the weekend, but that could result in too much screen time on any given day.

It's usually better to come up with non-screen rewards. Take a few minutes at a neutral time to jot down some of the things your children love to do or would love to do if they had the chance. These will make excellent alternatives to screen time as a reward. In my books *Calmer, Easier, Happier Parenting* and *Calmer, Easier, Happier Boys* I list examples of popular non-screen rewards. Here are some more, all of them tried and tested by parents who have committed to having one or more screen-free days every week:

gardening with a parent
ringing a grandparent
going on an errand with a parent without any siblings

the chance to use special art supplies

giving a concert or performance to the rest of the family

sleeping in a different room

choosing where he'll sit in the car or at a meal

planning the day's activities on a non-school day

money

moving the furniture around in his room (with parental
   supervision)

going shopping with a parent

eating out

Treats

I explained earlier that treats are nice things that happen occasionally; they don't have to be earned. Some screen time can fall into this category. For example, many families have a Family Film Night once or twice a month. As long as it doesn't happen every week, it won't add up to too much extra screen time. You wouldn't want to take the chance of one child being excluded from this cosy family event because he hadn't earned it. So make it a treat, not something that has to be earned.

The screen time reward plan limits the amount of screen time a child has. What about the other three screen issues?

Once you've decided on the maximum <u>amount</u> of screen time that each child can earn, you will still need to get clear about the <u>what</u>, <u>when</u> and <u>where</u> of the screen reward.

What

Allow only the content and type of electronic use that you have decided is good for your children. In order to be true to your values, you will need to be well-informed about what they're doing on their screens. Especially with teens and preteens, when you start investigating this, you may be horrified and appalled!

When

To simplify the family's rules, designate a time slot for screen time that has been earned. It needs to have a clear start time. Otherwise your children may rush through homework or meals to get to the screen. And it needs to have a clear end time, about two hours before lights out time. All of us, even our children, lead busy lives. You will probably need to designate different screen time slots on different days to accommodate everyone's activities and commitments.

Children, especially teens, will probably try to convince you that when they come home from school they need to relax in front of a screen before they can possibly face the dreaded ordeal of homework and music practice. Don't believe this! Yes, they do need to take some time to relax, especially if school was stressful, as it too often is. But as I mentioned, staring at a screen is not actually relaxing in the sense of refreshing. It is likely to make your child even less keen to get stuck into his homework, and he will do a poorer job of it. The screen activity interferes with several very important brain functions: concentration, mood and attention to detail. There are only a very few children who can have their screen time right after school and then come off it without a fuss, tackle their homework with a positive attitude and focus on doing their best. The chances are your child isn't one of this rare breed!

Even children and teens who don't make a fuss about homework and revision are usually not very motivated, after a long day at school, to do their best on their work. Screen time as a reward for homework done **to the parent's satisfaction** guides children, over time, into the habit of doing their best.

It may feel impossible to prevent screen use before homework, for example if your teenager comes home to an empty house several hours before you arrive home. I recommend putting parental controls on all available devices so that he can access only the amount of screen time he has already earned so far that day. And once an adult is home, the screen is switched off and real life takes over: homework and revision, music practice, helping to prepare the evening meal, chores, Family Time and Special Time (see Chapter 18).

Where

All the screen time that has been earned should take place in a common area of your house. In case you're worried that your child or teen would argue about this rule or simply ignore you, remember to tell him each day. That way he has to cooperate without a fuss in order to earn his screen time for that quarter.

CHAPTER 11

HOW TO INTRODUCE THE NEW PLAN TO YOUR CHILD

When you first tell your children that they will have to earn something that until now they were able to just take for granted, expect ructions! Don't assume they'll easily agree with the plan; that would be too much to hope for. When you first introduce the idea of having to earn screen time, you can expect one of four possible reactions:

Your child or teen may be outraged.
This highly pleasurable activity that she had been led to believe was her birthright has suddenly been transformed into something she has to work for – how dare you? She may cry; she may insult you; she may complain that it's not fair; she may threaten to run away and live with her best friend, where there are no rules. She may plead with you or sob hysterically. She may storm out of the house. She may declare that she will do whatever she feels like and you can't stop her.

As annoying as these over-the-top reactions are, we need to understand that the child or teen is experiencing a genuine sense of deprivation. You are talking about denying her easy access to something she has come to depend on, not just for entertainment but also for comfort. And children, especially those with a more extreme temperament, quickly learn that big reactions can often get parents to modify their original position. So I want you to take this dramatic reaction with a bucket of salt.

On the other hand, your child may act very blasé when you tell him the new screen time rules.
If he accepts your new plan with barely a murmur, you may be congratulating yourself on what a sensible, mature chap he is turning into. Maybe that's the case – but it's just as likely that he's taking it in his stride because he doesn't really believe you'll follow through. Perhaps he has seen other similar regimes come and go, so he knows that if he waits it out you will eventually forget to be consistent. Or maybe he has discovered that a lack of United Front between the parents keeps the earning plan from being implemented consistently. By all means Descriptively Praise your child (see Chapter 13) for staying calm in the face of these new restrictions, but don't be lulled into a false sense of security. This may just be the calm before the storm.

Another type of reaction comes from the budding lawyer.
This child instantly spots the loopholes in your new plan. She argues her case eloquently. She makes valid points, and you realise you didn't think things through carefully enough before you presented it a as new rule. She will lobby convincingly for exceptions.

Accept and acknowledge that you're human and fallible. Don't scramble to close the loopholes on the spot. You will need to give yourself some time to re-think these problem areas, and you will need time to reach a compromise with your partner, if you have one. So when your child flags up a potential problem, graciously acknowledge the shortcomings of your new plan, and set a date for when you will have ironed out the kinks and will let him know the amendment to the plan.

A fourth reaction that you might encounter is relief.
Some children and teens are acutely aware that they are
obsessed with electronics (even though they probably would
not use that word to describe themselves), and they know it
interferes with them spending time with the family or doing
their best on homework and music practice. They know that
screen time has largely replaced other leisure activities that
they enjoyed in the past. But they don't have the maturity to
know how to limit themselves. So they are relieved when the
decision is taken out of their hands.

How to handle the upset reactions

Thankfully, there is a lot we can do to minimise the initial
shock and outrage:

- Break the news to each child separately. You will be able
  to concentrate on one child's reaction at a time, and
  they won't be able to gang up against you.
- Choose a neutral time. That means a time when no one
  in the family is upset, in a hurry or in front of the screen.
- Have both parents present. The combined authority of both
  parents is very powerful. Your children will naturally take
  your new rules more seriously when you are demonstrating
  that you and your partner are a United Front. If for whatever
  reason it's not possible to have both parents there, ask a
  friend to support you. It will give you confidence, and it will
  show your children that you're not the only adult in the
  world who feels this way about screen time.
- Set aside more time for this meeting than you think you
  will need. You'll feel calmer and friendlier if you're not
  in a rush, and your calm, friendly attitude will help

defuse some (but not all) of your children's upset. Show, by your loving tone of voice and body language as well as your words, that you want your children to earn their screen time.

- Don't try to convince your child that this new reward plan is a good idea. Accept that the addictive nature of screens will probably blind her to that. When it comes to screens, it's as if children and teens are several years younger, in maturity and common sense, than their actual age.

- A child or teen with an extreme temperament may feel not only fury but panic at the news. In his distress he may impulsively blurt out whatever he thinks might get you to change your mind:

  'I hate you.'

  'You hate me – that's why you're doing this.'

  'If you try this, I promise I'll make your life a living hell.'

This is the screen dependency talking. He is not being rational when he is blaming and accusing and threatening, so don't try to reason with him when he's upset. A rational response from you will be useless at best, and it may actually exacerbate his upset. Instead of reasoning, justifying or arguing, keep Reflectively Listening (see Chapter 16):

  'It sounds like you're feeling awful about this.'

  'It could feel embarrassing, not being available on Instagram when all your friends seem to be on all the time.'

> *'I can see you're furious. Before you didn't have to earn being on the computer, and now you do.'*

- When your child or teen complains that *'Everyone else is allowed to . . .'* or *'Nobody else's parents make them . . .'* take a deep breath before you launch into a rebuttal. Whatever you say, no matter how true and wise your words are, she isn't listening! Don't say anything that seems critical of other parents. Don't even mention those (usually mythical) other parents. Wait for a pause, smile, give a hug if your child is not too angry to accept it.

  When you can see she's finally listening, you can say something like, *'My job as your parent is to make the rules according to what I believe is right'*. Over time this will sink in – but not overnight. In the meantime, carry on with the Reflective Listening (see Chapter 16). And keep talking about earning, not about 'taking away' or 'losing' screen time. If your child says 'take away' or 'lose', correct her each time by talking about earning. This will help her to shift to a more positive mindset, but probably not as quickly as you would like.

- Explain that you will make it easier for your child to keep up complete cooperation for a whole quarter by not springing instructions on her. Instead, you will give her a bit of advance notice that an instruction is coming so that she can prepare herself to cooperate the first time and without a fuss. The advance notice will consist of your going to stand in front of her.

- Give your child or teen a grace period of a few days or a week to get used to the idea of earning before you actually start the reward plan. Each day in the run-up to the start date, do a few one-minute *think-throughs* about the new rules (see Chapter 15). He may not want to do the *think-throughs* because he doesn't want to acknowledge to himself that this is really going to happen. But if you follow the guidelines for doing *think-throughs*, he will soon accept this new reality.

- Remember to Descriptively Praise (see Chapter 13) positive reactions to the new plan, for example any small instances of politeness, respect, willingness to listen, flexibility, courage, etc.

The good news is that whatever the initial reaction, if you commit to doing daily *think-throughs* and to using the other Calmer, Easier, Happier Parenting strategies I talk about in Section Three, your children and teens will accept your new rules, and they will make less and less of a fuss as the weeks roll by.

How you can help your children be more cooperative and earn their screen rewards

Complete cooperation for a whole quarter is not the same thing as perfect behaviour. Being a child and being human, before too long your child is likely to misbehave, in a small way or a large way. Complete cooperation for an entire quarter simply means that for those hours every time you give him an instruction, he does it the first time you ask.

Parents are generally amazed at how quickly the quarters system improves cooperation. You can hasten the process by not asking your child to cooperate when he's feeling uncooperative. For 'start behaviours' (when your child is not doing anything wrong, but it's time for him to start doing the next thing you want him to do), use the strategies in Section Three to help lighten his mood before you ask him to do something you think he might not want to do.

You may feel you can't possibly spare the time to jolly him into a better mood before you give your instruction. But let's remember how much time an uncooperative child can waste with whingeing, arguing, shouting, crying, storming off or just daydreaming and 'forgetting' what you told him to do. It's usually quicker to get him into a more cooperative mood before we give the instruction.

And if you find that you're often rushing so you can't possibly take the time to improve your child's mood, start earlier. Scheduling in plenty of time for a child to do things at a child's natural pace, without feeling rushed, usually improves everyone's mood immediately.

Before you give your child an instruction, tell her that you hope she'll do what you say the first time you say it so that she'll still be on track for earning her reward. Then, after you give the instruction, be willing to stand and wait about ten seconds longer than you would ordinarily wait for her to do what you ask. During that waiting time, your child is not only processing the instruction, but she's also thinking about the benefit of cooperating the first time you ask and about the cost of not cooperating the first time you ask. In Chapter 17 I explain about the Never Ask Twice method which is specifically for 'start behaviours'.

There will be times when your child is breaking or bending a rule or simply being annoying. These are called 'stop behaviours'. Here's how you can make it much more likely that he will cooperate and stop misbehaving the first time you ask so that he can stay on track for earning his screen time.

Instead of blurting out the usual 'No' or 'Stop' or 'Don't . . .', which are often ineffective, follow these steps:

1 At the first sign of misbehaviour, go and stand very close to your child.
Sitting does not convey the same seriousness and authority;

you need to stand. And proximity is very powerful. This step achieves three important things. It reminds your child that he's breaking a rule, in case he got so carried away that he forgot. It also reminds him that you're in charge. And he will see that you are fully aware of what he's doing. This first step usually results in partial or total de-escalation of the misbehaviour, in which case there will be something you can Descriptively Praise (see Chapter 13).

2 But if there's still some misbehaviour happening, now is the time to give an instruction, clearly, simply and only once.

Make your instruction be about what he **should do,** not about what he should stop doing:

> *'Hand me the hammer,'* is likely to be more effective than *'Stop waving the hammer about'.*

> *'Sit on the sofa now,'* usually gets quicker cooperation than *'Don't tease Fluffy'.*

Usually an instruction phrased in the positive will result in some improvement in the misbehaviour, so you will have something to Descriptively Praise.

3 If at this point some misbehaviour is still happening, don't repeat yourself or start explaining why strangling Fluffy isn't a good idea.

Don't threaten that he'll get no screen time for that quarter, even though it's true. Instead, take immediate and decisive action. The action you take will usually be removing an object from the child or removing the child from the situation.

Expect a tantrum the first few times you do this. Of course, because he didn't do what you said the first time, he won't have earned his screen time for this quarter, but now is not the time to volunteer this information. If he wants to know, ask him to tell you.

What happens when my child doesn't earn her screen rewards?

There will certainly be times when a child falls short of our expectations and doesn't manage to earn the full amount of screen time she could have earned. The first few times this happens, she may be bitterly disappointed. She may blame you; she may have a tantrum. But she will get over it, and she will learn that you are serious about your rules. Her habits will improve.

Don't ever respond to misbehaviour by taking away points or minutes already earned. What's earned is earned. Taking away something that has been earned feels grossly unfair and will erode trust.

All misbehaviour should be followed by a consequence that will motivate and help train, not one that just punishes. As you begin to put your screen time reward system into place, you will see how very effective the consequence for non-cooperation is. Your child simply doesn't earn all the screen time she was hoping to earn.

If you're nervous about a possible (or probable) negative reaction if your child or teen doesn't earn all the screen time she could have earned, you'll be tempted to overlook low-level misbehaviour or below-standard homework or cutting corners on chores. If you are desperate for your child to get all the screen time she could in theory earn, you may make excuses for her misbehaviour, or you may come up with a good reason why you should make an exception. If you do any of the above, your child will soon see that she doesn't really have to earn her screen time. So she will not respect the earning rule.

One thing that keeps parents from getting back in charge of a child's or teen's screen use is the worry that he simply won't accept that he now has to earn something that he previously thought of as his right. One mother put it like this:

> *'I thought Jamie would ignore anything I said and would just go ahead and do whatever he wanted. I'm a single parent so his father isn't around to back me up. I thought, "He's already taller than me. I can't actually make him do anything he doesn't want to do". I was afraid he'd make a huge scene. And he did! But I weathered the storm with lots of Reflective Listening and Descriptive Praise, and he came round.'*

We can maximise cooperation and minimise the upsets and the resistance by using the prevention and motivation strategies I talk about in Section Three, as the mother quoted above did.

We can also make it far more likely that even a child or teen with an extreme temperament will be cooperative (most of the time) by committing to improving the family's lifestyle. I give advice about this in my book *Calmer, Easier, Happier Parenting*.

How to deal with your child's screen dependency 'detox'

Because electronics are so addictive, it is certainly possible that your child or teen may become very upset when he doesn't earn all the screen time he was counting on being able to have. You're more likely to see a major negative reaction during the first few weeks of the reward plan, while he is still getting used to you being in charge. If you're practising the strategies that I recommend in this book, the massive tantrums that parents anticipate rarely happen. Quite quickly the Calmer, Easier, Happier Parenting strategies bring out the best in children and teens. These strategies result in <u>much</u> better behaviour and a much more sensible attitude. Until that happens, you may well experience some of these objections:

- *'You're treating me like a child.'*

  Even young children have been known to say that! This sentiment is often a sign that the child has been catered to too much, and as a result he thinks of himself almost as a quasi-adult: someone who has many of the rights and privileges of an adult, without, of course, any of the adult responsibilities.

  You can reply *'Yes, you're right. This new plan does treat you like a child. My mistake was that until now I treated you like you were older that you really are.'*

  Remember to keep a friendly smile on your face. Don't get sucked into arguing your case. You're the parent.

- *'No one else's parents have such strict rules.'*

  This is not likely to be true, but your child may actually believe it. Children and teens often lie to each other about what they're allowed to do at home because they're embarrassed to admit that they're not treated like grown-ups at home. And because so many children in the peer group are saying this, everyone else feels the need to keep lying to fit in with the perceived norms of the group.

  Your child may have a friend or acquaintance whose parents seem to be very lax about electronics, bedtimes, homework, etc. What your child doesn't see is the frustration and worry, sometimes even anguish and despair, of this 'lucky' child's parents. From experience, I know that many parents who allow children and teens the freedom to make unwise choices do not feel happy about it at all. They're doing it not because they think it's right, but because they've lost their way, and they don't know how to get back in charge. They're afraid of their child's reaction or afraid of trying to get back in charge and failing.

But let's imagine for a moment that what your child says is true, that your family is completely surrounded by a community of happily laissez-faire parents who really don't mind what their children do in front of a screen or when or where or with whom. You still have to be true to your values if you want to have any peace of mind.

It rarely improves matters if you reply, *'I don't care what other parents do'.* It sounds defensive and unfriendly, and it doesn't set a good example. We wouldn't want our children to reply, *'I don't care,'* when we talk to them, so we need to not use that phrase ourselves. And saying, *'I don't care,'* won't motivate your child to pay attention to you because she does care; she cares deeply about what her peers are doing.

You may be tempted to reply, *'Well then, why don't you go and live with them?'* It's rare (though not unheard of) for an angry child or teen to take you at your word and leave home just to get more freedom, but it does plant a seed, or it waters a seed that has already been planted. Even if your child doesn't seriously consider leaving home as an option, that response sounds as if you don't really care if he stays or leaves. Instead, we need to Reflectively Listen (see Chapter 16) to what the child is really feeling, below the level of his words: *'It sounds like you're really upset about our new rules.'*

- *'This is stupid.'*

This just means your child is upset about the new rules. Don't get drawn into arguing, justifying, reasoning, lecturing, cajoling. Instead Reflectively Listen:

'Sounds like you're angry.'

'Maybe you're wishing things could stay the way they were.'

- *'If I can't have my phone, I won't know where my friends are going to be.'*

This is a very legitimate worry because nowadays many teens, and even some pre-teens, are in the habit of making plans with their friends through texting and social media. Naturally your child doesn't want to feel left out of arrangements. That's why your screen rules need to take this into account. He will still be able to communicate with his friends, but it won't be whenever he feels like it any more; it won't be during the times each day when screens are off-limits.

- *'This is going to be so embarrassing.'*

As I have mentioned, we all need to feel we belong to a group that welcomes and appreciates us. In earlier generations that group was the extended family, but now it is the peer group. Of course kids worry that if they do something that their peer group perceives as 'uncool' or 'sad' they risk rejection, either subtle or blatant. We need to accept that children and teens probably will feel embarrassed at first, until they see that others of their peers also live with screen time restrictions and until they become less addicted.

- *'I wish I had cooler parents.'*

You can probably remember feeling like this, back in the day! What teens and preteens mean by this and similar statements is that they wish you treated them as if they were more mature. Don't waste your breath explaining that you'd be glad to trust them with more freedom if they behaved more sensibly. It will come across as a lecture, a nag or a criticism, and it won't motivate them to be more mature. Instead, let's accept that many children naturally feel this way. We can Reflectively Listen (see Chapter 16):

'You're probably feeling really angry about these new rules.'

'Maybe you wish we'd forget all about these rules and let you play on your Xbox for as long as you want.'

- *'I hate you.'*

This also calls for Reflective Listening (see Chapter 16). But it may not be easy to focus on Reflective Listening if you're feeling hurt and misunderstood. You know that you are trying your best to be a good parent, and you know it isn't easy. You may feel angry at your child's lack of appreciation for everything you do for them. Remember that your child's negative reaction is so strong because screens are so addictive. It's almost as if he's not in his right mind in that moment when he's blurting out those hurtful words.

- *'I'm not listening.'*

As much as you may want to, don't reply with *'You better listen to me, young lady, if you know what's good for you!'* Instead, Reflectively Listen (see Chapter 16):

'*Maybe you're so angry you don't even want to think about what I'm saying. I'll tell you more about the new rules later.*'

- '*I won't do it. And you can't make me.*'

Don't respond with '*Yes, I jolly well can make you. Just watch!*' Remember that when children say '*I won't*', it's an impulsive blurt, not the result of a carefully thought-out plan. It's similar to a toddler screaming '*No!*' We know better than to take a toddler's refusal seriously; we know that in a while he will calm down and forget all about how upset he was.

Of course, older children and teens have longer memories than toddlers, so their upsets can last longer. But if you commit to using the Calmer, Easier, Happier Parenting strategies, you can transform reluctance and resistance and even outright refusal into cooperation. At first the cooperation may be surly and half-hearted, with muttered insults, possibly even some swearing, especially if you have a teenager. You will get lots of testing to see if you're going to stand firm or if, to avoid a scene, you will look the other way while he bends or ignores the new rules. Sooner or later, and to parents' surprise and delight it's usually sooner, your child's mood will lighten because he is 'detoxing', becoming less addicted.

At home and away: What to do when other families don't share your screen values

When you first start contemplating the logistics of limiting exposure to electronics, you can easily get overwhelmed. A common worry is how to cope with peer pressure, which can feel as uncomfortable for parents as it does for the children. You <u>can</u> get back in charge of electronics and stay in charge, even if you are surrounded by families with different values and different screen habits.

Here are some typical scenarios that will probably come up, followed by my suggestions for how to handle the differences in screen habits between your family and another family.

If you and your children are going to visit a family with more lenient screen rules than your own (or no rules at all)

You have several options:

- You can let the other set of parents know in advance that you have new rules at home. Explain that you would like to stay as consistent as possible outside the home as well. It will probably take some courage to overcome your embarrassment and say this, especially if you are worried that the other parents will think you're odd, too strict, too controlling, old-fashioned, etc. That's a possibility. They might think all those things about you, but they'll probably be too polite to say so.

  What's more likely is that the other parents will be impressed by your determination. They might even take strength from your stance and feel inspired to take steps of their own towards getting back in charge of their children's screen use. But what if you simply can't face saying what you want?
- You can tell a white lie and say that your children are looking forward to doing something specific at their house – building a fort in the garden, playing Monopoly, playing with Lego, etc. Request that time be spent doing this before any screens are switched on.
- You can plan to visit the other family at a time of day when the children are likely to be playing outdoors.

- You can suggest that you all go to a nearby park first.
- You can say, whether it's true or not, that your children are likely to get crabby if they have too much screen and not enough time burning off their excess energy outdoors.
- What doesn't work is to ask or tell your children not to get involved in the screen activities that are happening all around them. That's asking for an unrealistic degree of self-control.

If you don't feel strong enough emotionally to bring up this potentially thorny issue in advance, you can simply say nothing and allow the other family's lifestyle choices to prevail. This option can be very appealing, especially if you're worried about giving offence.

But there are some downsides to this decision. You may have a hard time relaxing and enjoying yourself if you see your children stuck in front of a screen, absorbing the values of your hosts. And the break in consistency may interfere with the new screen routines you've been focusing on establishing. Also, for many children the more exposure to screens they have, the more likely they are to become overexcited, over-reactive, grumpy and uncooperative. This is unpleasant enough when it happens in the privacy of your own home, but it can be mortifying when it happens in front of other people.

If a family (or a child) with different screen habits is coming to visit your family

- Remember that you are completely in charge of what happens in your home. You don't need to cater to someone else's screen preferences.
- If you suspect that the visiting family won't automatically fall in line with your screen rules, it's only fair to

warn them ahead of time. Without apologising or justifying, explain your plan for screen time. For example,
the plan might be to give the children half an hour on
the Playstation after playing in the garden for an hour.

Usually the other parents will be too polite to protest,
even if they think your approach to electronics is wrong.
(Grandparents and extended family, however, may not
be too polite to object!)

- You can, as in the earlier scenario, focus on how much
your children are looking forward to doing a specific
(non-screen) activity with their children. Screen time
will come after that.

If your family are staying with another family overnight

In this situation, it would be unrealistic to expect the host
family to change their screen habits.

- You can of course decide to go along with whatever the
other family is doing, which might include not only too
much screen time or inappropriate computer games, but
possibly also later bedtimes than you would like and too
much junk food. This approach can work if your children are quite easy-going and their behaviour is not
likely to deteriorate significantly.

But going along with routines that don't bring out the
best in your children will probably lead eventually to your
telling them off when really their negative reactions are
not at all their fault. And if you have a child with a sensitive or inflexible temperament, going along with the other
family's lifestyle can store up trouble for when you get
back home and want to re-establish your routines.

- It usually makes more sense to Prepare for Success (see

Chapter 15) by deciding in advance which rules and routines you are willing to modify and which you aren't. Be brave; stand up for what you believe is right. Make sure to prepare your children for having to go to bed earlier than their friends, for having to spend some time doing their homework or revision, for eating more healthfully and for going to the park even if their friends are glued to a screen all afternoon.

Screens and playdates

Parents worry that their child's friends won't want to come to the house for playdates if there are screen rules. This is especially a concern when a child is unconfident or has an extreme temperament. Here's what one mother did:

'Ben was in tears when I told him that from now on all playdates at our house have to start with real playing, and then they can go on the Xbox for the last hour. He was sure his friend would think he was babyish and weird. Part of the problem was that Ben thought he was rubbish at traditional games. I felt so sorry for him that I almost changed my mind. But instead, my husband and I gave him lots of practice at playing games – Uno, Monopoly, Upwords, draughts, some word games – so that he would feel more confident. Then during the playdate I supervised the game to make sure Ben was staying friendly and polite. Both boys had a great time! And I felt great that I stuck to my plan.'

CHAPTER 12
Q & As

Q: *This screen time reward plan seems very rigid. What's the harm in being more flexible?*

A: Of course you can make occasional exceptions to your usual screen limits. If the World Cup is on, no one would expect your child to switch off after one hour. If he's at the cinema, you won't expect him to leave in the middle of the film. But keep the exceptions to a minimum. Otherwise after a while they won't feel like exceptions; they'll feel like the norm. And don't make exceptions in response to pleading or pestering. Once your child sees that those tactics work, you'll get lots more pleading and pestering.

Q: *The big problem in our house is the meltdown when it's time to come off the screen. How can I teach my children to accept the rules?*

A: We can also use the power of routines to help children and teens deal with something that can feel awful to them: the moment when they have to tear themselves away from Screen World and re-enter the real world. I recommend this strategy. It's not a magic wand, so it may not result in instant cooperation without a fuss. But very soon you'll see, and hear, less and less fuss. Set two timers to go ding five minutes before the screen time will be over. Your child keeps one of the timers with her. If she's young and likely to fiddle with it, put it out of reach but still visible. That way she can check how much time she has left. You keep the other timer with you.

When the timer goes ding, you and your child both know that she has five more minutes. Go to her and spend the next five minutes talking about whatever is happening on the screen. If necessary, give her a countdown at five minutes, then at four minutes, then at three, etc.

If you simply announced that she had five more minutes and then you left the room, it would be as if you had never spoken, so when you came back in five minutes your child would be just as surprised or resentful. But because you're staying with her for the last five minutes, she can't block out the fact that her time is almost up. In fact, she's likely to start winding down even before the five minutes are up.

Here's another way to use routines to ease the transition from screen to non-screen. Establish the habit of a special book or game or activity that you do with your child right after he comes off the screen. This probably won't be necessary after the first few weeks.

Q: *During the week, my children are very busy so they probably wouldn't have time for more than about an hour of screen time anyway. But at the weekends they've got bags of time so of course they'll want more than one measly hour. Won't they need more screen time to fill up those empty, unstructured hours? Otherwise I'll be hearing endless complaints of 'I'm bored!' and 'There's nothing to do'.*

A: For many children, preteens and teens, being on a screen has become the default position, the activity that they automatically drift towards when they're not sure what to do with themselves, when there is some free time between activities, when they are not being entertained and when they want to relax.

Maybe you're worried that your kids would be bored because they would have nothing to do. You might be feeling sorry for them, or perhaps you want to spare yourself their whingeing and pestering. As I mentioned earlier, it's never true that there is nothing to do. It's just that the screen dependency makes it feel as if no other activity could be as much fun as screen time.

Let's remember that from the dawn of history until about seventy years ago, people, old and young, relaxed without screens. How did they do it? They relaxed by hanging out with family and friends, by playing card games and board games, by kicking a ball around, by going for bike rides, by stamp collecting, by helping with cooking and shopping and gardening and cleaning out the garage. They read, they drew and sometimes they just sat on the sofa and stared into space. All of these are extremely useful activities. They are relaxing, and they are good for us.

So there's no need for your children or teens to have extra screen time on non-school days. If you add in Family Time, Special Time and independent play (see Chapter 18), your children will have an enjoyable, full day without needing extra screen time. But if you do decide to allow more, don't give too much more; it won't be good for their moods, their minds or their bodies.

Q: *Is there really any point in making screen rules? I'm thinking my kids would quickly find a way round the rules. They could go to their friends' homes to play computer games, or they could borrow a friend's device and I'd be none the wiser.*

A: Here's a solution to the problem of your child spending lots of time at friends' homes where access to screens is unlimited. Make a rule that the location of the playdates has to alternate between your house and the friend's house. Your child may not like this rule at first, but using the strategies from Section Three will soon take the sting out of it.

If you are concerned about your child bringing home a device he has borrowed from a friend, or indeed has bought with his own money, remember that you will know about it pretty soon. You will either see your child using it, or you will notice he is spending a lot of time in his room or in the loo. At that point you can relieve him of the device and put it in the drop-zone with all the other devices. And as I said earlier, the strategies in this book will help reduce the upset and will guide your child or teen into more sensible habits.

Q: *My son is so much cleverer with computers than I am. How can I make sure he won't manage to get around the parental controls?*

A: Parents can feel like 'digital immigrants', outsmarted by their children, who are the 'digital natives'. It's a truism that children are far more comfortable with technology than their parents are. Even when children don't know how to access something on a computer, they have an idea of what might work, and they're not afraid to experiment.

Luckily, parental controls are getting tighter all the time. But often the problem is not so much that children and teens are hacking into the parental controls software as that parents are not taking basic precautions, like putting passwords and timers on all devices, removing remotes, dongles and leads when not in use, keeping devices under lock and key.

In case you hate the idea of having to be this vigilant, you'll be reassured to learn that you won't have to take these extreme measures forever, just while your child is 'detoxing' from screen cravings. Once you establish the twin strategies of limiting and earning and you reinforce them with the supporting strategies in Section Three, children and teens will become less and less fixated on electronics. They will start to develop more sensible habits. Week by week, you will be able to trust them a bit more and then a bit more.

Q: *We're a family of five, and my kids love technology and have all sorts of gadgets. How can I keep track of all their devices?*

A: You will see them lying around. As you come across them, gather them up. Soon you will have all the hand-held gadgets in your possession, ready to dole out at the appropriate times and for the appropriate length of time. And soon all the bigger screens will be in a public place.

Q: *There are so many great documentaries on TV. I wouldn't want my children to be deprived of them. And I play educational games on my phone with my kids. It's a cosy, calm family activity. I don't want to give that up. The problem is I don't know if that's what they would choose to do with their screen time if it were limited.*

A: You don't need to give up that cosy time or the documentaries. If you believe your children would benefit from (rather than simply enjoy) a particular screen activity, you can arrange for this to be a treat, quite separate from the screen limits or rewards.

Q: *Sometimes we get home too late for the children to have their screen time, even though they've earned it. We get cries of* 'It's not fair!' *What should we do?*

A: If it's not your child's fault that time ran out, then he shouldn't be penalised. The screen time he has earned can be saved for the weekend. Don't let him have it on a school night because school nights are busy enough as it is. Have him spread out the extra time over the weekend, no more than one hour at a time, with activity breaks in between. This is much better for his brain than staring at a screen for several hours in one go. If this problem of running out of time is happening more than once a week, you will need to look at your schedule and plan more realistically.

But maybe the reason there wasn't enough time was partly due to your child wasting time by dawdling, arguing, wandering off instead of doing what he was told. In that case there should be no rollover. Expect your child to be upset, and don't try to reason him out of how he is feeling. Instead, Reflectively Listen (see Chapter 16):

'You were really looking forward to Club Penguin tonight. I can see how disappointed you are.'

'Maybe you're wishing you hadn't used up the time by lying on the floor when it was tidy-up time.'

Q: *I've started using screen time as a reward, and my teenage boys are accepting it pretty well, except for one thing. At the weekend, they love to play online games with their friends for hours at a time. So they want me to let them 'bank' the screen time rewards they've earned during the week so that they can have one long marathon session at the weekend. Would that be very bad for them?*

A: Long periods of time in front of a screen aren't good for our moods, our cognitive functioning or our muscles (especially those of the eyes, core and back). But once a week you could give your sons a bit more of what they want, maybe extending the time period to two hours at a time, rather than limiting it to one hour. They may or may not be grateful for that concession!

I also suggest that you get into the habit of doing more

with your sons at the weekend, as a family and also one-on-one. You can use the power of routines to change their habits, in this case the habit of how they spend their free time. Parents are often busy at the weekends with errands, DIY, home maintenance and paying bills, while children and teens are playing – often in front of a screen. Turn your tasks into Family Time and Special Time (see Chapter 18). Involve your boys, together or one at a time, in your weekend activities.

There may be some initial resistance, but persevere. Praise their efforts. You will find that soon your sons will be lapping up your undivided attention. They will be enjoying doing something grown up, they will be learning useful life skills, and they will feel good about themselves because they are being helpful.

Q: *How should we handle it when the children aren't with us for some of the quarters? We won't know if they've been behaving well or not.*

A: If you're concerned that your child might not have been cooperating, you can usually get a report from a supervising adult, for example the football coach or the parent at a play-date or sleepover. Make it clear to your child in advance that you will be checking up on her cooperation. This gives her the chance to make an effort to earn the reward for that quarter.

If you feel it would be too awkward to ask the adult in charge, or if you want to spare your child the possible embarrassment, you can simply give your child the benefit of the doubt and assume that he earned his screen time for that quarter of the day. You will also need to do this if there is no adult you can ask, for example if children are playing unsupervised. And if your child usually cooperates, you can safely assume that he earned his reward for that quarter.

Q: *My daughter is very temperamental, a real drama queen. When she hasn't earned her computer for one of the quarters, she cries and pleads with me to give her another chance to earn it. She promises to be extra-good. Is it OK to give her a second chance?*

A: When parents set up a reward system for screen time, they may be dreading the fallout if the reward isn't earned. They really want the child to earn the daily or quarterly rewards. This could be because she has a sensitive, intense or inflexible temperament, and they can't bear the thought of the fuss they are sure she would make if she didn't earn all her screen time. Or maybe the parents really believe that her tears and sobs mean she is suffering terribly. No, she's just upset.

Whatever the reason, if you are desperate for your child to earn the reward, it's easy to set the bar too low or to overlook many instances of minor non-cooperation or to make exceptions and excuses. This is a mistake. If she doesn't need to make much of an effort to earn her screen time, it won't seem to her as if she really has to earn it. The earning will just be a rubber stamp.

And parents won't have the use of this very effective motivator for guiding their child into better habits regarding homework, bedtimes, sibling interactions, tidying, etc. And because screen time will still feel like a given to the child, on the rare occasions when parents actually do put their foot down and follow through and she doesn't earn her screen time, she will feel very resentful. It will feel as if something that is hers by right has been cruelly ripped away from her.

A frazzled or guilt-ridden parent may try to avert a tantrum by giving the child a second chance to earn what she didn't earn. Don't even think about it! If she didn't earn it but gets another chance to earn it, she doesn't need to take it seriously that she didn't earn it. In order for the rule about earning screen time to do its job of motivating children to improve their behaviour and habits, there needs to be no negotiating, no deals or bargains, no fudging. If she didn't earn it, she didn't earn it. She won't have to wait too long before the next quarter of the day happens and she can earn the next bit of her screen time.

Q: *I'm worried that if my daughter misbehaves at nine o'clock in the morning and realises that she won't earn her reward for that quarter, she won't have any incentive to behave. Do we really have to be that strict?*

A: This reward system does not expect children to be perfect. In a quarter of a day of course there's likely to be some misbehaviour. What we're focusing on for the reward is cooperation, following instructions the first time. So as long as she stops the misbehaviour the first time you tell her to, she's still on track for earning her reward.

But there's another important point I want to make. The chance to earn screen time is not the only, or even necessarily the most important, reason why children get into the habit of cooperation and then self-reliance. Children (even teens) want to please their parents. When we show that we're pleasable, and when we say exactly what actions please us, children will do more and more of those actions. The reward is just a little something extra to ease your child over the hump of her initial resistance.

Q: *My son sometimes does the exact opposite of what I've just told him to do. Then he has a tantrum because he didn't get his reward. How can I get him to see that if he just cooperated, he'd get to watch the programmes he loves?*

A: Sometimes a child seems to deliberately sabotage his chance to earn the next bit of screen time. Parents want to know what drives this child to jeopardise the screen time he seems to be so desperate for. There are a number of possible reasons:

- When children are hungry or tired, they are more inclined to deliberate or impulsive misbehaviour.
- When Special Time isn't frequent and predictable (see Chapter 18), a child may be so fixated on getting the parent's attention that he temporarily forgets all about earning or not earning screen time.
- Children with a particularly intense temperament can get hooked on the excitement of testing to see if they can make a parent cross. This can easily be as much fun as screen time.
- If parents have not been consistent about following through, the child may not really believe they will stick to the rules about not having earned screen time for that quarter.
- An angry child may go into revenge mode. His urge to annoy or upset the parents by misbehaving is even stronger at that moment than his desire for screen time.

I suggest that you tackle all the factors from the above list that apply to your child. It may feel too overwhelming to decide to address all of the relevant factors at the same time, but this will result in much better behaviour very quickly. If you can't face making lots of changes all at once, pick one or two from the list that you feel will have the most impact on your child's motivation and confidence.

Q: *My son keeps asking me, probably twenty times a day, 'Have I lost my screen time?' It's driving me mad. Help!*

A: There are several issues to address here. From your question, I can hear that your son is still thinking of screen time as something he automatically starts out with but that you can take away from him if he misbehaves.

Everyone in the family, parents and children, needs to get into the habit of thinking about screen time as something that has to be earned. To change from a mindset of losing something you start out with to a mindset of earning something you don't start out with, we need to be careful about the words we use. Let's discipline ourselves to use the words that reflect the concept we're trying to get across. To guide our children to think about screen time differently, we will also need to correct them when they talk about *'losing'* or *'taking away'*. We will do it gently, but we need to do it. You might reply to your son:

'Are you wondering how much screen time you've already earned today?'

'Do you want to know if you'll still earn your screen time for this morning even though you grabbed the book from your sister?'

When he answers, you can say, if it's true, *'So far you've done everything I told you to do since you woke up. And you gave the book back to Hannah when I told you to, and with no whinge-ing. So far you're earning your screen time for this quarter. Keep up the good work!'*

It's usually useful to explore why something that we don't like keeps happening. We'll often get a clue as to what needs to change and what we can do to change it. So let's think about why your son keeps asking you this question so many times every day:

- Maybe he doesn't quite understand the screen time rules. If you do lots of *think-throughs* (see Chapter 15), soon you will be confident that he understands them thoroughly.

- Perhaps there's been some inconsistency and this has confused him. The solution is to focus on following through consistently and to get united with your partner, if you have one.
- Maybe you're being too vague about what he has to do to earn his screen time: *'Be good'* or *'Have a good attitude'*. He won't ever be quite sure if he was good enough to earn the reward so he's likely to keep checking.
- It could be that he's used to being told off or to seeing an exasperated look on your face, so he can't really believe he's managing to earn the reward. The solution is to give him lots of Descriptive Praise (see Chapter 13) and to smile more. And each time he asks, think of it as an opportunity to point out to him what he's been cooperating about.
- Maybe it's just a way he's discovered to get you to engage with him, and he's become stuck in a rut of talking only about that. The solution is twofold. First, make sure he's getting frequent Special Time (see Chapter 18). Second, make a rule for yourself that you will only talk about what he has or hasn't earned at certain times, for example at the end of each quarter.

Now let's talk about how to handle your son's question if he hasn't been completely cooperative during the quarter. You may be reluctant to speak the truth if you're expecting a barrage of whingeing, arguing or shouting. Be brave! If you have started putting the Calmer, Easier, Happier Parenting strategies into practice, he will move through his upset more quickly than he would have in the past.

You can start with lots of Descriptive Praise (see Chapter 13):

'You had almost complete cooperation this morning. You got out of bed the first time I asked. You let go of the box when I

*told you to let Hannah serve herself. And some things I didn't
even need to tell you to do. You put your bowl in the dishwasher, and you took your lunch bag out of the fridge. But
there were two things you didn't do the first time I asked.
You tell me what they were.'*

In case you're thinking that you wouldn't have the time to
say a long paragraph like this, you can tell your son that
you'll talk about it later. That would be preferable to giving
him a quick *'No, you didn't earn it,'* which would leave him
angry and would teach him nothing.

Q: *What happens when one of the children has earned their screen
time but the other hasn't?*

A: Keep the sibling who hasn't earned it with you so that he
isn't partaking of the other one's screen time. If you think he
might refuse to stay with you, that's a cooperation issue.
Before you tell him to stay with you, give him advance notice
that you're about to give him an instruction. Tell him that
you hope he will cooperate the first time so that he'll still be
on track for earning his screen time for this quarter. And do
lots of Reflective Listening (see Chapter 16):

> *'It probably feels awful having to stay in this room when you
> know Alex is in the other room on the computer.'*

> *'Maybe you're wishing we didn't have these rules.'*

Q: *My teenager has had a computer in his bedroom for a few years,
and he spends hours up there, ignoring the rest of us. He's furious that now we're saying he can't. Every day he argues about
it and shouts and refuses. How can we get him to accept the
new limits and earning rules?*

A: Just because your son is stuck in some counterproductive habits, that doesn't mean you have to abandon all hope of getting back in charge. But achieving this won't be quick or easy.

It can be tempting to just make a rule. But we should only make rules that we can follow through on; otherwise all we are doing is advertising our weakness.

You will not be able to use screen time as a motivator if he already has access to his computer whenever he wants. But usually there are other motivators that teens will work for or behave well in order to get. One of these is money. So you could make a rule like, *'Each day that you keep your screen switched off after nine p.m. you'll earn a certain amount of money the next day'*. Another good motivator for teens is being able to be with their friends. You could say, *'Each day that you do your homework in the sitting room instead of in your bedroom, you can earn getting to go out with your friends for a certain number of hours at the weekend'*.

I hope you noticed that in the above examples I phrased the rules in terms of what he should do, not what he shouldn't do, and I talked about rewards rather than about consequences. Talking about consequences makes everyone feel bad. Talking about consequences reinforces your teen's view of himself as someone who is doing things wrong all the time. Talking about rewards makes everybody feel better, more hopeful.

I am not suggesting for a moment that these extrinsic rewards are all you will need to get an addicted teenager back on track. Rewards are an extra little sweetener that boosts motivation. But be aware that if your teenager is very angry, at first he may well get more satisfaction from upsetting you by breaking the rules than he would get from earning rewards by following the rules.

Rewards will only be effective in a home environment in

which parents are practising being positive, firm and consistent. It will take a lot of self-discipline on your part not to rise to the bait when your teen is being disrespectful. You will need to steel yourself not to try to avoid arguments by doing things for him that he could do for himself. And you will need to spend some enjoyable Special Time with him every day (see Chapter 18), even when you're so annoyed with his attitude that you don't even want to make the effort to be friendly.

Q: *A few months ago I heard you give a talk at my children's school about getting back in charge of screen time. It sounds good, but to tell you the truth, I haven't started it yet – even though I've threatened it a few times! I've got so many questions about exactly how to do it. What will happen if I do it wrong?*

A: Maybe you can't imagine yourself in charge, or maybe you're not even sure that you have a right to be in charge. If that's how you're feeling, please re-read Section One; that should reassure you that everyone in the family benefits when the parents get back in charge.

Maybe your worry is mostly about how your children will react. Start with the assumption that they will be upset, and then you'll be pleasantly surprised if they're not. Section Three will give you lots of strategies for easing children and teens over their initial anger and resistance.

All those questions you have about exactly how to put this plan into action in your family – you will never have all the answers! Re-read Chapter 1, which is about how to get in charge, and then dive in and get started. You'll have lots of opportunity to tweak and self-correct along the way.

Q: *This screen time reward plan seems like a lot of work. Will I have to keep it up forever?*

A: Some of the strategies I recommend in this book will feel harder than others at first. But with consistent practice, all these strategies will get easier and easier. They may never become so automatic that you don't even have to think about them, but they will become second nature.

And as you get into better habits, so will your children. As you see more sensible habits emerging, it's tempting to think, *'Job done! Now I can take my focus off electronics'*. That's a fairly common mistake. Through all our children's growing-up years, until they leave home and often beyond, we continue to focus on the things that matter to us: our children's education, their health, their emotional well-being. Electronics impacts all of those things so we will need to keep monitoring it. But as your children's screen habits improve, there will be less and less you need to actually do; it's always easier to keep a ball rolling than to start it rolling.

Q: *My son doesn't seem that fussed about technology. I don't think screen time as a reward would really motivate him. When I've suggested the idea of earning, he says he doesn't care. Should I do the earning plan anyway?*

A: Maybe he really doesn't care, or maybe it's his way of getting you to not bother starting the earning plan. Or maybe he's so used to having his screen time that he can't really imagine that he wouldn't still automatically get it. Whatever the reason, I recommend that you get started, first with using the power of routines to limit screen time, and then with the earning plan. If cooperation is not a problem, he'll be earning most of his screen time most days anyway. Make a point of noticing whether he remembers to use the screen time he's earned or whether he truly doesn't care.

Even if your son is not interested in screens now, this may

well change in the future. So it makes sense to get him into good habits sooner rather than later. If cooperation is a problem, you can think of the earning plan as an experiment. And if you think your son would be motivated by different rewards, arrange for him to be able to earn those as well as the screen time. A very effective reward for many children is getting to play with a favourite toy for an hour or so, eg Lego, certain toy cars or trains, art supplies, a particular doll. They could even earn getting to wear a much-loved item of clothing.

Q: *Do I really need to use rewards to get my children into good habits?*

A: You don't have to use extrinsic rewards, i.e. things or activities. If what I'm suggesting doesn't fit with your values, don't feel you have to force yourself to do it. Especially if you have a very easy-going child and if you're already in the habit of being very positive, firm and consistent, you can establish sensible habits simply with routines and with Descriptive Praise (see Chapter 13), which is also a reward, although not a tangible one.

THE CALMER, EASIER, HAPPIER PARENTING STRATEGIES THAT WILL MAKE THE NEW SCREEN HABITS EASIER TO ESTABLISH

CHAPTER 13
DESCRIPTIVE PRAISE

Whenever I explain the new screen rules and routines to parents, I get reactions like these:

'How am I going to get my kids to go along with the new plan?'

'I can't stand it when my children argue about the screen rules and try to find loopholes. I want some respect.'

'I don't want to have to keep repeating myself.'

If your child doesn't even look up when you tell him to switch off his device, or if he says, *'In a minute,'* for the fifth time, it's easy to start fuming and to decide that what's needed is a consequence. Surely a consequence will motivate him to do what he's told? Consequences do have some uses, and I will explore that in Chapter 17 when I talk about *action replays*. But most consequences don't guide children or teens into better habits.

For many parents, lack of cooperation is the most frustrating part of parenting. Luckily it's never too late to guide our children into the habit of first-time cooperation. But it won't be a quick fix.

Instead of lecturing and telling off when our children do something wrong, what's much more motivating is to praise them when they do something right. But this is easier said than done because humans are more inclined to notice what's wrong in a situation. It takes self-discipline on our part to notice and mention when children are <u>not</u> misbehaving, such as <u>not</u> whingeing, <u>not</u> interrupting, <u>not</u> shouting, <u>not</u> insulting, <u>not</u> squabbling, <u>not</u> grabbing, <u>not</u> arguing about the rules.

Descriptive Praise is about noticing and mentioning the little OK things our kids do, the sorts of things we hardly register because we feel we should be able to take good behaviour for granted. This strategy is called Descriptive Praise because we describe exactly what the child did right or exactly what he didn't do wrong.

The screen time reward plans I talk about in this book highlight cooperation (children doing what they're told, the first time and without a fuss) and self-reliance (children telling themselves the right things to do, rather than needing to be told each time). So cooperation and self-reliance are two very important habits we want to strengthen through Descriptive Praise.

Make a point of Descriptively Praising the little instances of cooperation and self-reliance that you see throughout the day, as well as the other qualities that you want to see more of, such as friendliness, flexibility, helpfulness, attention to detail, courage. Don't tell me you can't find any! Look carefully and you will find some instances of good behaviour every day.

Here are some examples of Descriptive Praise for little bits of cooperation. The more you say things like this, the more cooperation you will get:

'I asked you to sit down, and you came straightaway.'

'You got your pyjamas out of the drawer when Mum told you to.'

'You heard me say no more biscuits so you didn't take any more.'

Here are some Descriptive Praises that will result in more self-reliance and a more mature sense of responsibility:

'You got dressed and made your bed before you came down for breakfast.'

'I saw the two of you sharing the markers, and there was hardly any arguing.'

'Just now when your sister spilled her juice, you didn't laugh.'

Here are some examples of Descriptive Praise that are specifically to do with screen time:

'Every day you're arguing less about the new computer rule.'

'A few minutes ago when Harry came and stood in front of the screen, you didn't push him out of the way. You shouted at him, but you didn't hit him, even though he was teasing you.'

'You gave me your tablet the first time I asked you for it.'

'This morning you didn't ask for the iPad before school. You're remembering our new rule.'

In case you think you can't say these kinds of praises to your teenager, you can! He might sometimes find the Descriptive Praise embarrassing because he wants to think of himself as someone who's already doing everything right. But the Descriptive Praise will still be effective.

I'm sure you noticed that in all these Descriptive Praise examples, the parents weren't saying, *'Well done'* or *'Brilliant'* or *'Terrific'*, which is how people usually praise before they learn about Descriptive Praise. It seems natural to say those superlatives because we're so used to talking like that. But one problem with the superlative praise is that it's so vague. The child is often not really clear what he did that was so great. There isn't any useful information in that type of over-the-top praise. Praise is much more effective when we're very specific. And often those superlatives aren't even accurate. A lot of the time parents are saying 'Fantastic' about something that's basic good behaviour, not anything fantastic.

Each time you say a Descriptive Praise, you're helping your child to see herself in a new, more positive light. This makes it easier and easier for her to be more cooperative, and then eventually self-reliant, about all the things you want her to do, including following the new screen routines. You can use Descriptive Praise to improve any behaviour that's problematic. I challenge you to say ten Descriptive Praises a day to each of your children. You'll see that Descriptive Praise brings out the best in children and teens.

Because Descriptive Praise is a very different way of showing our appreciation and approval, parents often have lots of questions about this strategy. For a thorough exploration of Descriptive Praise, please read *Calmer, Easier, Happier Parenting*.

CHAPTER 14

STRENGTHENING YOUR RESOLVE

Getting back in charge of electronics <u>can</u> be done, and it's worth doing. But it's a big job, and it won't always be easy or fun. There are bound to be times when you will need to call on every ounce of positivity and determination you can muster. We have all experienced how tempting it is, when we are stressed, exhausted, irritable or preoccupied, to snap at our children, to shout, to threaten or lecture – and to give in.

You can make the job of getting back in charge easier and more enjoyable by taking care of your own needs first. This is similar to what the cabin crew on airplanes keep telling us: put your own oxygen mask on first, before you attempt to put one on your child. Otherwise you risk running out of oxygen, and then you can't help your child at all. In this chapter I want to talk about a few 'oxygen masks' that will help you feel less stressed so that you can keep up your emotional strength; you will need it to get back in charge of the technology in your home.

Getting enough sleep

I am asking you to commit to reducing your levels of everyday stress, not just because you deserve a less stressful life, but also because your children deserve parents who are less stressed. In order to honour this commitment, the first thing we need to do is get more sleep. Lack of sleep (even one hour less sleep a night than the ideal) is stressful for our bodies, our minds and our emotions. But we're so used to this chronic, subtle sleep-deprivation that it feels normal. We've almost forgotten what it feels like to wake up rested.

The accepted wisdom is that adults need at least seven hours of sleep a night. But only thirty years ago, the recommendation was for eight hours of sleep a night. Obviously our bodies have not suddenly evolved to need an hour less sleep a night. What's happened is that experts are aware that nowadays eight hours sounds hopelessly unrealistic so they are hesitant to recommend that.

If you are currently getting less than seven hours a night, make a promise to yourself to get at least seven. You should start feeling better within days. Getting the television out of the bedroom will help you get into this habit of going to sleep earlier and will set your children a good example too! Once you're regularly getting seven hours a night, go for eight. That is really what your body and brain need for optimum functioning: for buoyant energy, clear thinking and a cheerful mood. You will love how you feel. And you will be much more prepared to take on tough challenges – such as getting back in charge of the electronics in your kids' lives.

Learning how to be less stressed

Most adults in Britain spend a couple of hours each evening in front of a screen. This is meant to be relaxing, but it actually makes people more stressed. This is partly, but not entirely, due to the content people are being exposed to: murder, rape, wars and natural disasters on the news, and more of the same in television programmes and films.

But even if you watch only films and programmes about animals, gardening, house makeovers, period dramas, etc, where the content is soothing or uplifting rather than upsetting, the time you spend sitting in the same spot, hardly moving, is the opposite of what your body and brain needs.

If you're like most parents, your end-of-day screen time is soaking up an average of one to three hours that could be devoted to activities that are more fulfilling and therefore more truly relaxing and restorative. This may sound obvious, but the outcome of any truly relaxing activity should be that we end up feeling refreshed and replenished, calmer, more positive, energised. But that is not what happens when we settle ourselves for our nightly screen time: television, film viewing, playing games online or surfing the web.

Probably the screen activity does take your mind off your worries or your to-do list temporarily; this is an important reason why becoming absorbed in what's happening on a screen can be so habit-forming, for adults as well as for children. But the relaxing effect is very short-lived. This is partly because end-of-day screen viewing is usually so passive, both physically and mentally. We evolved to enjoy using our bodies and brains to overcome challenges. And research confirms that leisure activities that involve moving, creating and imagining are powerful de-stressors. Here is a list of hobbies and pastimes, alternatives to screen time, that many parents have found to be truly relaxing activities:

- reading or listening to audio-books
- catching up with distant family and friends, via telephone, FaceTime or letter-writing
- games like cards, chess, Scrabble, etc
- cooking or baking
- DIY
- gardening (indoors or outdoors)
- keeping a journal or writing a blog

- singing, listening to or making music
- movement – dancing, yoga, stretches, weights, trampo-lining, sports, etc
- drawing, sketching, painting, crafts
- collecting
- learning a foreign language
- meditating
- taking a long, hot bath or shower
- and last but not least, chatting or cuddling with your partner

There are of course many other de-stressing activities. They will all give you a sense of satisfaction that is missing when we watch a television programme or film, no matter how excellent, or when we play a computer game, no matter how entertaining.

You will feel better – more rested and more energetic physically, mentally and emotionally. You will have greater reserves of determination, very necessary for dealing with whingeing, blaming, pestering, insulting and other forms of disrespect. You'll be able to stay calmer and more positive when your children test your new screen time rules, as they certainly will at first.

If you're like most people, every once in a while you start (or re-start) doing some of these activities, and you have the best intentions of getting into a constructive routine. But if you're chronically sleep-deprived, you will probably lack the motivation, willpower or emotional energy to keep going with your de-stressing activities once the initial excitement has worn off. Ironically, when we're already feeling stressed due to low-level sleep deprivation, it can feel even more stressful to think about how we could organise our lives differently in order to become less stressed.

Many parents have told me that at first it takes a strong and sustained effort of will to commit to becoming less stressed. But parents are usually willing to undertake this once they understand that the best gift they can give their children is a parent who is less stressed. This goal motivates parents to challenge and overcome the initial inertia and reluctance.

CHAPTER 15

PREPARING FOR SUCCESS

Preparing for Success is an umbrella term for a set of strategies that will make it easier and easier for your children to get into the habit of following your rules and routines without having to be told each time, including the screen time rules and routines. In Chapter 8 I talked about how you can prepare the environment to minimise resistance and to maximise cooperation and self-reliance. In this chapter I will explain a new and very important strategy called a *think-through.*

Establishing rules and routines

A rule tells children exactly what they need to do and what the consequences will be when they do it right or when they do it wrong. We need rules when we are dealing with potentially problematic behaviour, whether minor or major. The purpose of rules is to create routines. A routine is what is happening when your child or teenager is already in the habit of doing what you want him to do. We need rules and routines to help establish a wholesome lifestyle for our children and teens so that they can mature sensibly.

A lot of what parents think are rules in their house are not really rules. A rule needs to be clear, and it needs to be phrased in terms of what the young person should do; it is not enough to talk about what she should not do. And a rule needs consistent follow-through. Otherwise it isn't a rule, it's just a nag; inconsistent follow-through increases the likelihood of resistance the next time. That is because there is a side of human nature that leads children and teens to want to take risks. They want to see if there is a chance that they can avoid the consequences of your rules; that feels quite exciting.

We can look at the family as a micro-climate, a little valley, safe and protected, surrounded by tall mountains that keep out storms. Rules and routines are the mountains, the barriers between your family and the outside world. Rules and routines enable you, the parent, to be true to your values within the protected micro-climate of the family.

There are a few myths I need to dispel about rules. One is that children and teens hate rules. At school and in their extra-curricular activities, children and teens follow lots of rules without giving the matter a second thought. What children and teens do hate is parents getting angry when the rules are broken. They also hate inconsistent follow-through. Another myth is that if parents make rules and follow through on rules, children and teens will become rebellious. Experimentation is part of growing up, but rules actually help stabilise behaviour and values.

Often we're so busy and distracted that we only remember to mention a rule after it has been broken. The least effective way to transmit our values is with lecturing and telling off after something has already gone wrong. When we react after the event, we will probably be annoyed or disappointed or even shocked, and that kind of reaction makes teens and preteens not want to listen to anything we have to say. Instead, we need to Prepare for Success before things go wrong.

We need to prevent as much misbehaviour as possible so that our children and teens get into good habits. I'm sure you have heard the expression, *'An ounce of prevention is worth a pound of cure'*. We can focus on prevention by establishing rules and routines and then following through to make sure the rules and routines are being followed. We can give

children and teens small bits of responsibility and then monitor them closely.

Using *think-throughs* to establish rules and routines

We establish our rules, which soon become routines, with a
very effective technique called a *think-through*. This is not blaming or scolding; it is not lecturing or justifying or arguing. A
think-through is a friendly conversation that lasts one minute. It
is structured in a particular way. You will ask your child or teen
some questions about what the rule or expectation is and what
she should do, and she will answer your questions.

Let's say that the rule you want to insist on is that your child
needs to finish his homework before he can have any screen
time. Rather than repeating and reminding or exploding in
frustration and irritation after things go wrong, a *think-through*
is an extremely positive way of getting your point across.

The name *think-through* is a bit of a tongue-twister, but my
hope is that it will remind you not to keep doing what hasn't
worked in the past. I hope it will remind you that you need to <u>think</u>
carefully to decide which questions you will ask your child or teen
about the rules and routines, and he will need to <u>think</u> carefully
about how to answer your questions accurately and thoroughly.

First choose a neutral time; this means a time when neither
you nor your child is upset, and neither of you is in a hurry to
get somewhere. And of course neither of you is in front of a
screen. During the one-minute *think-through* you don't talk
about what he did wrong the last time or about what he should
not do. You phrase the new rule in the positive. You might
say, *'The new rule is that from now on you need to finish your
homework to our satisfaction before you can go on the computer'*.

State the new rule in one simple sentence, and then refrain from explaining and justifying; it will only annoy both of you. If he wants to know why you've made this new rule, ask him to take a sensible guess. You'll find that he knows. Children generally understand why they are supposed to do the things we ask of them. Having told him the new rule, you then ask *think-through* questions like:

'What's the new rule that I just told you?'

'What do you have to do before you can go on the computer?'

'What does "to our satisfaction" mean?'

These questions are going to seem extremely odd to your child, and he may not feel like answering them at first. Here's why it's so important that he answers your *think-through* questions. When he tells you <u>what</u> he should do and <u>when</u> he should do it and <u>where</u> he should do it and <u>why</u> he should do it, he is automatically visualising himself doing it. This is very different from if you were reminding or lecturing, which is so unpleasant that children try not to listen. The more often you are willing to do these *think-throughs,* and the more thorough his answers are, the more vivid the image in his brain will be of him doing the right thing.

And pretty soon something quite amazing will happen. If you keep doing the *think-throughs,* within a few weeks, and sometimes within just a few days, your child's brain will automatically transfer that image into his long-term memory. This is so remarkable because the long-term memory is the repository of habits, but simply by answering the *think-through* questions, this new image of your child following the screen rule will become lodged in his long-term memory, just as if it is a memory of an action he has done many times. Once this image is in his long-term memory, it feels like a habit so it will be easier for him to do it right without even giving it much thought. It just happens naturally, the way habits do.

Only state the new rule before the first *think-through*. For subsequent *think-throughs*, assume that he will remember the rule or routine. If he says he doesn't remember, tell him to take a sensible guess.

Research into how the brain works has revealed that it is necessary to focus one's mind on a piece of information for a minimum of eight seconds in order for the brain to be able to transfer that information into the long-term memory. This is why children and teens need to answer our *think-through* questions thoroughly, so that they are spending at least eight seconds at a time visualising themselves doing it right.

Commit to doing a few *think-throughs* a day. However, if you have a big problem, it needs and deserves a big solution. And a big solution would be ten *think-throughs* a day. This intensive intervention is very effective. If you, and your partner if you have one, commit to doing ten *think-thoughs* a day about whatever rule or routine you want to emphasise, you will find that within just a few days your child will be doing it right ninety percent of the time.

You may be assuming that your child, and especially your teen, would hate having to do *think-throughs*. Usually kids don't mind at all because you're being friendly and positive. But it's possible he might not like it, as it reminds him that this is a habit he needs to improve. But he probably won't hate it. What he probably would hate a whole lot more is the old way – you repeating, reminding, telling off, an impatient tone of voice, threats, maybe even shouting.

If there are two parents in the home, both should take responsibility for doing the *think-throughs*. Your children will take the rules much more seriously if you do *think-throughs* with both parents at the same time. For boys it is important that fathers ask a lot of the *think-through* questions because boys naturally look up to their dads, want to be like their dads and want their dads to be proud of them. Let's harness this natural instinct.

Parents worry that a tricky or moody teen will refuse to do these *think-throughs*. This is very rarely a problem. The *think-throughs* are happening at a neutral time, not when you or they are annoyed, so there is no scolding involved, no frowning, no impatience or irritation in your voice. And each *think-through* lasts a maximum of one minute. It's not an ordeal! And let's remember that our children and teens answer their teachers' questions all day long without making a fuss. You deserve the same respect. Your teen can be just as respectful to you, and this will happen as you put all the Calmer, Easier, Happier Parenting strategies into practice.

It's quite possible that during the first week or two of this new strategy, your child or teen may test you to see if you're going to follow through or give in. She might complain:

'This is so boring!'

'But I answered all those questions this morning. Why do I have to say it again?'

'You're so patronising.'

Here's where we need to control our own frustration or anxiety. It's understandable that our children will be grumpy or disrespectful if that has worked in the past to get a rise out of you. So stay calm (at least on the outside).

It doesn't matter if the *think-throughs* are boring. We mustn't act as if boredom is going to kill our kids. They can survive being bored for one minute. If your child complains that she already answered the same question yesterday, you can say, *'Yes you did tell me. And you'll need to tell me again. We'll have these think-throughs every day until I see that you're remembering the new routine'.* When kids complain that *think-throughs* are boring, what they usually mean is you are systematically closing off their options for ignoring you, and they would rather not be pinned down to following the rules. When kids say you're being patronising, usually it just means that they would like to think of themselves as someone who is already mature and doesn't need any further training. So persevere. The more *think-throughs* you do, the sooner your children and teens will get into good habits.

Children learn how to annoy parents by acting foolish or downright stupid. When you ask a question such as, *'What do you need to do before you can have your screen time?'* your child might reply, *'I don't know'*. Don't believe her; of course she knows. But there's no point in getting annoyed because that would sidetrack you from your job, which is teaching and training with the *think-throughs*. Whether you believe her or not, a really good response is, *'Take a guess'*. Even if she doesn't have a clue what the answer should be, she can always take a guess. If your child is particularly resistant and angry she might respond with, *'But I really don't know'*. You can say, *'That's OK. You don't have to know; you just have to take a sensible guess'*.

Remember that each *think-through* lasts no more than one minute. So if a minute is up and your child still hasn't taken a guess, just say, *'OK, the minute is up. I'll ask you again in a little while,'* and then just walk away. This will feel uncomfortable for your child because she knows she should answer you properly. After all, she answers her teachers properly.

If you're willing to walk away from rudeness and foolishness, the likelihood is that quite soon she will come to you wanting something. She may ask what's for dinner, or she might want your help to find something or fix something. She might want to complain about something, or she might want to tell you a joke she heard or some interesting snippet of news. But really what she wants to do is to reconnect because children, even teenagers, want to be in communication with us when we are being friendly. So when she comes to you wanting something, you could say, *'I'll be glad to talk with you about that after you answer my questions'*. And at that point she probably will answer your *think-through* questions because you're not angry with her so she doesn't have much reason to be angry with you. Also, she can see that nothing else is going to happen until she finishes the *think-through*.

Internet safety and *think-throughs*

Children and teens have heard again and again from parents and teachers and magazine articles all about how to stay safe on the internet. But they think they are invincible. They can't imagine that anything bad could ever happen to them, so they often don't pay attention to sensible guidelines. Another reason they don't absorb and remember and follow all that good advice is that reading and listening are the least effective ways of learning and remembering.

Think-throughs are much more effective. Have your children tell you what the rules for sensible internet use are. *Think-through* questions always start with WH: who, what, where, when, why, which (and how).

Be prepared to do weekly *think-throughs* about internet safety, long after it no longer seems necessary. Teens continue to need frequent, ongoing guidance and supervision even though they don't think they need it, even though they may argue and push against it.

You may not believe that the *think-through* strategy could possibly influence future behavior as rapidly as I'm saying it will. You don't have to believe me. Challenge yourself to do several *think-throughs* every day (each one takes only one minute), and you will see the results for yourself.

CHAPTER 16
REFLECTIVE LISTENING

Most children and teens will balk at the new screen time rules and routines at first. Of course we want to transform their resistance into acceptance as quickly as possible to prevent most of the complaining, arguing and shouting (from us as well as from our children). How we often respond when children are upset, with telling off or reasoning or justifying, doesn't usually work to help children feel better or behave better. Descriptive Praise, *think-throughs* and rewards are far more effective.

Here I'm going to introduce another very useful strategy that helps children and teens to feel better and behave better. This is Reflective Listening. When you learn about this strategy and commit to using it every day, you will have an invaluable resource for minimising the inevitable conflicts over electronics.

Reflective Listening is a way of reacting to upsets that's different from what we usually do. Ordinarily when children or teens are showing us by their words or by their tone of voice or behaviour that they're upset about something, we try to set them straight, appealing to their reason. The problem is that when children are upset they're usually not open to listening to reason. Trying to convince a child or teen that what she believes is wrong and that what she's feeling is unreasonable is not likely to get you anywhere. In fact, it may make her even more upset and resistant.

When you Reflectively Listen, you do something completely

different. You don't try to make your child see sense. Instead, you focus on trying to understand the painful emotion your child is going through and on showing that you're trying to understand.

Your child will feel comforted when he can see that the most important people in his life, his parents, are taking the time to think about how he feels. You might not think we would need to go out of our way to demonstrate to our kids that we care about their feelings; surely they know that, don't they? But because we so often focus on the annoying behaviour that accompanies upset feelings, it can seem to our children as if all we care about is their behaviour.

When children feel heard and understood, the intensity of their upset will gradually fade, even though the situation they're upset about hasn't changed. They move out of being stuck in their uncomfortable emotion. As a result, they're more open to problem-solving, and they're more likely to listen to your pearls of wisdom — as long as you keep it short.

Another benefit of Reflective Listening is that over time it will teach your child a vocabulary for expressing her feelings so that she won't feel the need to misbehave to try and get you to see how terrible she feels.

Reflective Listening has four steps

Step One

First we need to pause so that we don't automatically react in our usual (and often unhelpful) ways. We need to set aside our own upset so that we can think clearly. This may not be easy to do because a child's or teen's upset is often accompanied by disrespect or some other form of misbehaviour, which parents naturally find upsetting. But if our old ways of reacting are not working to build better habits, we need to do something different.

Step Two

Next we need to listen. We need to give the child our full attention without jumping in with our opinion or with suggestions. Let's show we are listening by stopping what we are doing and by looking at him. We can make listening noises, such as *'Umm . . .'* or *'Ah . . .'* Of course you can give your child a hug if you feel that might help.

Step Three

We mentally put ourselves in the child's shoes, and we try to imagine or guess what he is really feeling below the surface of his words. We need to look deeper because children are often confused or inarticulate; often they don't know how to express what they really mean.

We use our words to reflect back to the child what we imagine he is feeling. The name of this strategy, Reflective Listening, comes from this important step.

Here are some examples that are related to the new screen rules:

- You're playing chess with your child during Special Time (see Chapter 18), and he says, *'I hate this game. This is so boring'.* There's no point in telling him that he'll enjoy the game more as he gets better at it, although this is probably true. Here's what you might say if you're looking below the surface:

  'You're not used to spending time alone with me, playing. Maybe it feels uncomfortable.'

'I'm guessing you'd rather be on your phone right now.'

- You tell your child or teen that he's earned half of the screen time he could have earned, and his angry response is *'I don't care!'* He wouldn't react like that if he didn't care, so you could say:

  'Probably you're wishing you'd earned the full amount.'

  'I'm guessing you're angry about the new screen rules. You liked it a whole lot better when you could go on your computer whenever you wanted.'

- You tell your child that in five minutes it will be time to switch off the screen, and he shouts, *'You just want to ruin my fun!'* Rather than arguing with him or saying, *'Don't be ridiculous,'* you could Reflectively Listen:

  'Looks like you're really disappointed that you'll have to watch the end of that video tomorrow.'

  'It's not easy to stop playing when you're having so much fun.'

  'It sounds as if you're really angry with me right now.'

Step Four (optional)

Another way to Reflectively Listen is to give your child his wishes in fantasy. This injects a note of lightness and fun:

- On a long journey, when your son complains, *'I'm bored. I want my iPad,'* you can say, *'Wouldn't it be great if we could just click our heels and instantly we'd be home, like Dorothy in the Wizard of Oz'.*
- When he whinges, *'I want to finish this game,'* you could say, *'Maybe you wish you could play on the computer for as long as you like, and no one would stop you'.*

If you give your child his wishes in fantasy, he will feel understood and heard.

I've given examples that are related to the new screen rules and routines you're establishing, but of course there will be plenty of other things that happen that your children will find upsetting. Use Reflective Listening whenever your child is upset, instead of lecturing and telling off, and also instead of giving in.

You may find that Reflective Listening isn't easy to remember to do at first. It's not our habitual way of reacting when things go wrong. But persevere with it; you will soon see that your children and teens are becoming more emotionally resilient.

CHAPTER 17

IMPROVING COOPERATION WITH THE NEVER ASK TWICE METHOD AND ACTION REPLAYS

We want our children to earn the screen time rewards we are offering so that they start to see themselves as cooperative, self-reliant, successful, well-behaved, focused, kind, etc. The more cooperative and self-reliant your children are all day long, the more cooperative and self-reliant they will be about the screen issues. So it makes sense to give our instructions in a way that will make it more likely that they will do what we ask the first time and without a fuss.

As I have mentioned, the things we ask our children to do fall into two categories: 'start behaviours' and 'stop behaviours'. There are many times every day when our children are not doing anything wrong, but we have one eye on the clock, and we want them to move on from what they are doing in order to start doing the next thing on our agenda. These are 'start behaviours'. When a child or teen is breaking a rule or bending a rule, that's a 'stop behaviour'.

A minority of children are naturally compliant. These tend to be children with a very easy-going temperament; even when they have to do something they don't much want to do, they're not likely to get very upset. And their upsets blow over very quickly. But for most children, cooperation is a habit we need to teach and train.

Of course we would like our children to respond as soon as we give an instruction, but often they're so absorbed in what they're doing that they barely seem to hear us. And even when they do hear, they don't want to stop what they're doing.

It can be infuriating when children don't pay attention to what we tell them to do. It's easy for parents to drift into the habit of repeating, pleading, cajoling, bribing, telling off, threatening . . . and eventually maybe even shouting.

To establish this important habit of cooperation we need to show our children that we mean what we say, and that they do need to follow our instructions, even when they would rather be doing something else.

The Never Ask Twice method for 'start behaviours'

In most households on any given day there are far more 'start behaviours', so that's what I will talk about first. The Never Ask Twice method will guide your child into the habit of doing what you say the first time you say it, even when he doesn't feel like it. This is a friendly, respectful method – and it's very effective.

The Never Ask Twice method has six steps. Most of the time you will only need the first three steps. But there will be times when your child is more resistant. The remaining three steps will help transform reluctance into willingness.

A word of warning: don't give your child an instruction while he's having the screen time he's earned. We've all seen how immersed children become when they're staring at a screen; they may not even realise that someone is talking to them. So to Prepare for Success, all screen activities should happen only after children have completed everything they have to do, from homework and music practice to tidying their belongings and household chores.

Here are the six steps of the Never Ask Twice method:

1 Stop what you are doing, stand near your child and look at him.
If your child is not yet in the habit of first-time cooperation and you ask him to do something without first going to him and giving him your full attention, he's not likely to pay much attention to you. For example, when you're telling your child that she has to tidy her room before she can watch television, you may barely look up from chopping the onions or sending an email. Don't be surprised then if an hour later she still hasn't done what you've asked.

2 Wait until your child stops what he is doing and looks at you.
You need to get your child's attention before giving your instruction so that he will take you seriously. We often under-estimate the time it takes a child or teenager to shift his thoughts away from what he is doing and to start concentrat-ing on what we are saying. Once your child is looking at you, it is harder for him to pretend he didn't hear you. Steps One and Two show that we respect the child. We are treating our child as calmly and politely as we would treat a friend or a stranger. Children respond much more positively to a friendly, calm approach.

3 Give the instruction – clearly, simply and only once.
Giving the instruction only once is important. If you give in to the temptation to repeat yourself, your child automatically won't have earned his screen reward for that quarter, and it won't even be his fault. Also, your child will see that he doesn't

need to do what you ask the first time you say it. Instead, he will learn that he can wait until you start nagging or becoming upset.

You can make it easier for your child to transition from what he's enjoying doing to what you want him to start doing. In Step Three give him a five-minute countdown. The key is to stay with him for those last five minutes and to show an interest in what he's doing. Chat about what will be happening next, which will help him to visualise himself moving on to the next thing you want him to do.

Most children most of the time will cooperate after Step Three, if you've remembered to do Steps One and Two. As soon as he starts to cooperate, remember to show your appreciation with Descriptive Praise.

But in case he hasn't made a move in the right direction, proceed to:

4 Ask your child to repeat the instruction back to you – accurately, thoroughly and in his own words.
Once your child has told you in his own words what he should do, you both will know that he has heard and understood. He is more likely to do what you have asked after he hears himself saying what he needs to do. Most of the time this is all that is necessary to get cooperation. Remember to Descriptively Praise!

But if your child is digging his heels in, go to the next step:

5 Stand and wait.
Standing conveys authority; we are showing that we are in charge and that we mean what we say. Standing and waiting demonstrates that we are determined to follow through; we're not getting distracted and we're not giving up. At this point your child will probably get up and do what you've asked. Even

if you're feeling annoyed because you had to wait, Descriptively Praise that he's now cooperating. But if he hasn't yet started to cooperate:

6 While you're standing and waiting: Descriptively Praise every step in the right direction, no matter how small. Also Reflectively Listen to how your child might be feeling about what you have just asked him to do.
The Descriptive Praise is very important. It sends your child the message that you still like him and that you are confident that he <u>will</u> cooperate. Staying positive and Descriptively Praising are not easy to do at first. It's not what we are used to doing!

With Reflective Listening we show that we care about his feelings, not just about his behaviour. For example, we can say that he seems cross that he has to put his Lego away. This helps him to feel understood.

Here are some frequently asked questions about the Never Ask Twice method:

Q: *What if my child doesn't do what I ask after Step Three or Four? I don't have hours to stand and wait for him.*
A: When you use the Never Ask Twice method, it's rare for children to refuse to cooperate. When you stay calm and positive, children and teens naturally become more and more willing. Usually what makes children angry and defiant is a parent's annoyance and telling off. But when parents aren't nagging, lecturing and blaming, most kids want to do the right thing.

It's true that if your child is not yet in the habit of first-time cooperation most of the time, at first this method may well take longer that you would like. So I suggest that you pause for a moment before giving your child an instruction in Step Three. If you sense from his mood that he may not want to do it, spend a few minutes helping him to feel more willing. Both Descriptive Praise and Reflective Listening are useful for this; so is a hug. And make sure you have the time to follow through with all six steps, in case this turns out to be necessary. Over time, your child will see that you really do follow through until he cooperates, so he will cooperate more and more quickly – most of the time!

Following the Never Ask Twice method might result, the first few times, in your child being late for school, or your not having time to prepare dinner or having to postpone an errand. All these situations are inconvenient, but they are much less important in the long term than guiding your child into the habit of first-time cooperation. Eating sandwiches for dinner for a few days because you didn't have time to cook, or even a few days of your child arriving late for school, are not going to damage you or your child. But a child who does not easily cooperate will present more and more problems as he grows into a teenager and then a young adult. You'll need to invest some time and effort in the short term in order to benefit yourself, your child and your family in the long term.

Q: *Does the Never Ask Twice method always work?*

A: Yes, this method always works, if you don't give up. I have never seen it fail. This is because <u>all</u> children and teens want to please their parents, as long as we stay friendly and calm. Another reason this method always works is because there is no Step Seven that says: after a while, give up.

The Never Ask Twice method should be used only when you are sure your child knows how to do what you have asked. If you want your child to do something she cannot do or thinks she cannot do, then she will need some support from you. The Never Ask Twice method is designed to address lack of cooperation, not lack of skill. If your child lacks the skill to do what you've asked, you will need to teach her how to do it.

For example, teachers sometimes set homework that is too difficult. If a child is not confident that he can write a good history essay, or if he doesn't know how to answer a maths question, he needs some guidance. Just insisting that he get on with it will not usually work.

Q: *What do I do if my child storms out of the room after I ask him to do something he doesn't want to do?*

A: Don't go after him. If we follow him around the house, we are letting him lead us. Instead, we need to be in charge!

We cannot force a child to do what we want at any specific moment. But sooner or later, and usually sooner, he will come back to you wanting something. You can then say that you will be glad to talk about whatever he wants to talk about as soon as he does what you have asked him to do. Over time, by using the Never Ask Twice strategy, you will influence him and guide him into the habit of cooperation.

Q: *I know that in Step Six I need to Descriptively Praise my child. What can I praise when he's not doing what he should be doing?*

A: Descriptively Praising a resistant child isn't easy at first. It's not what we feel like saying! However, Descriptive Praise does usually work to shift a child's mood and improve his willingness.

We can praise every tiny step in the direction we want. We might say:

'You're sitting in the right place,' when he is sitting on his chair but not yet doing his homework.

'You're holding your jacket,' even though he hasn't put it on yet.

We can praise past good behaviour:

'Yesterday you did everything I asked you to do, with almost no arguments.'

'You know how to keep your room tidy. In fact, you've kept it tidy for almost a week.'

We can praise the absence of negative behaviour:

'Even though you don't want to empty the dishwasher, you're not being rude.'

'It looks like you're worried you won't like this new food, but you're not pushing your plate away.'

When Descriptively Praising the absence of negative behaviour, we should only mention things that the child sometimes does wrong. For example, if your child is rarely rude, or never pushes his plate away, we will need to find something else to Descriptively Praise. Otherwise it might sound insulting.

Q: *Do I always need to go through all the six steps?*

A: Always start at the beginning with Step One. Eventually most children most of the time will follow your instruction as soon as you give it (Step Three). All you need to do then is praise them for following your instruction without any argument.

After a while many children will do what they are supposed to do even <u>before</u> you say it because your presence (Steps One and Two) is enough to remind them of the usual routine, and they just go and do it. Of course, once a child does what he should do, you don't need the remaining steps.

Q: *My child often knows exactly what he should do next because we have the same routine every day. How can I teach him to do it on his own, without my having to tell him each time?*

A: If you're pretty sure your child knows what he should do next, instead of giving the instruction in Step Three, you can go straight to Step Four: *'What do you need to do now?'* If he says he doesn't know, ask him to take a sensible guess.

Action replays for 'stop behaviours'

One of the defining characteristics of a rule is that something happens when the rule is broken. Without a consequence it is not a rule; it is just a nag. I would like to introduce a completely different way to approach consequences. Based on my experience and observation, the usual consequences are not effective at getting kids into good habits. Consequences show children what we don't want them to do, but too often children are able to avoid consequences by not getting caught or by convincing the parent that there was a good reason for what they did.

Consequences do have a limited value. Consequences may get your child's attention; they may show you are serious; they may help curb your child's impulsivity. But most consequences do not teach or motivate. Here's a little saying I made up: *'If consequences worked, our prisons would be empty.'*

Here's a very effective consequence; it's called an *action replay*. If you are willing to commit to doing an *action replay* after every incident of misbehaviour, whether tiny or huge, very soon you will see more and more cooperation and self-reliance and less and less misbehaviour and negative attention-seeking.

Don't start the *action replay* while your child is still upset. Wait for him to calm down, which could take five seconds, five minutes, occasionally much longer. While you're waiting for him to calm down, you can Descriptively Praise and Reflectively Listen, or give him a hug, but don't chat or play with him, as that would distract him and dilute the message that a consequence is needed for his misbehaviour.

Once he's calm, do the *action replay*, which has two parts.

The first part is asking him what he should have done differently. Once he tells you properly, the second part is that he shows you what he should have done.

Here's an example: let's imagine that one evening you tell your child that there won't be any screen time tonight, even though he has earned it, because traffic was very heavy and you all got home too late. If your son reacts by calling you an insulting name, that would constitute misbehaviour. As soon as he stops insulting you, wait about five seconds and then Descriptively Praise him for stopping. I know this isn't our usual response to rudeness, but Descriptive Praise when he stops insulting you gets the point across that he shouldn't call you names far more effectively than a telling off would.

Once he's calm, you could say, *'When you were disappointed that you couldn't have your screen time tonight even though you had earned it, what should you have done instead of calling me a name?'* If you've waited until he's over his upset before you ask him this, he will probably reply sensibly, perhaps by saying, *'I should have said OK'*.

Now that he has the image in his head of himself doing the right thing, you move on to the second part of the *action replay*. You might say, *'We're going to act this out now so that you can show me the right way to behave. Listen while I say again what I said: "We got home so late tonight that there's no time for Doctor Who." Now I'm listening to what you say.'* And he'll probably say *'OK'*.

Action replays improve behaviour rapidly because the child is getting practice at doing things right. And the last memory he will be left with of any incident is the image of himself doing it right. This helps him over time to see himself as someone who (mostly) does the right thing. This positive self-image leads to better and better behaviour.

You may like the idea of doing an *action replay* for every little bit of misbehaviour, but you may have lots of questions about the details. I explain *action replays* in depth in two of my earlier books, *Calmer, Easier, Happier Parenting* and *Calmer, Easier, Happier Boys*.

CHAPTER 18
REPLACING SCREEN TIME WITH OTHER ACTIVITIES

We've seen that when too much screen time becomes the norm, children become less interested in non-screen activities. So during the early weeks of this new screen time reward plan, you may find that your children and teens don't know what to do with themselves. All children at every age are capable of entertaining themselves (even infants in a cot play with their fingers), but if they haven't been left to entertain themselves, they may forget how and may then resent being expected to relearn this basic skill.

Most parents want their children to develop and sustain an interest in a broad range of activities. We know that different types of activities hone different skills, teach different values and bring different types of enjoyment and satisfaction. Also, we don't know how a child's gifts and talents will unfold, so we want to give her a chance to explore different possibilities.

So it can be upsetting for parents when children and teens start complaining that everything, except electronics of course, is 'boring' or 'uncool'. Teens in particular become more and more absorbed in Screen World and less and less enthusiastic about activities they used to find enjoyable and fulfilling.

Parents often assume there is nothing they can do to influence this worrying phenomenon. We may not be able to reverse this trend completely because the teen (and increasingly preteen) subculture, where electronics is the main activity, is so influential. But there is a lot we can do to re-awaken interest in non-screen pastimes and hobbies. Even for teens and preteens, spending time with parents is an effective antidote to screen obsession. But of course the time the family spends together needs to be enjoyable. When time spent together as a family is more enjoyable, one important result is that children, even teens, will absorb your values, which probably include not giving up on real life, not getting sucked into Screen World.

You may need to put some time and thought into planning some alternative activities to screens. These can be part of what I call Family Time and Special Time. Family Time is one or both parents with two or more children, doing something you all enjoy. Special Time is one parent with one child. First I will talk about Family Time.

Replacing screen time with Family Time

Family meals

The most common Family Time activity is having meals together. Research has shown that there are many benefits to the whole family sitting down for a meal together on most days. Children become more articulate and better informed about general knowledge and world events because they hear more adult conversation. They enjoy school more, get better grades and are more likely, eventually, to graduate from university because they are exposed on a daily basis to their parents' interest in their education. Siblings get along better because they have to practise being civil to each other for a period of time every day. Their table manners improve, as well as their willingness to be more adventurous in their food choices. Even surly teens start to lighten up and enjoy Family Time.

Teens are less likely to experiment with minor or major wrongdoing (missing school, cheating, stealing, drugs, irresponsible sexual activity, reckless driving, aggression) because they are absorbing their parents' values every day. They spend less time in Screen World as they shift their allegiance back to the family. So make sure family meals happen every day, if at all possible, with no screens allowed.

Some family activities to enjoy

Here are some activities that parents have found useful for reducing children's screen cravings. Most of these activities are very versatile and can be adapted to be suitable for any age, which means that younger and older siblings can be involved at the same time. These Family Time activities use inexpensive materials and supplies that you are likely to have on hand or that are easy to find:

- Lego
- arts and crafts: as children get older they often decide that they're 'rubbish' at anything artistic. Parents have found that making collages is a way to sidestep this pernicious belief because this activity requires no special skill or talent
- board games
- word games
- nature hunts in the garden
- treasure hunts
- listening to music together
- reading to your children

These are activities that can be enjoyed by all family members of all ages: children, teens and parents. But you may be convinced that your surly teen or preteen would turn his nose up at such uncool activities. My advice is: persevere. Even teens will re-bond with you, and after a while they won't be so concerned about keeping up their image of themselves as worldly or sophisticated.

If your child is very angry about the new screen rules, you can expect him to be highly resistant at first, declaring that any activity you suggest (other than screens) is babyish, boring or stupid. If he doesn't want to participate, get started on the activity on your own or with a sibling. Children love to hang out with parents who are in a good mood and who are making time for them. So he will probably gradually inch his way over towards you, especially if you show that you're having fun, but without trying to convince him that he'll have fun. An angry, resistant child may delight in proving you wrong.

Reducing sibling squabbles with Family Time

Spending time together as a family can be enjoyable and rewarding, or it can be very stressful. One factor that can make all the difference is whether siblings are getting on well, without lots of bickering or competitiveness. Parents may be so used to the sibling squabbles that they can't really imagine a peaceful atmosphere that lasts for more than a few minutes at a time. In fact, this is one reason parents give for allowing more screen time than they know is good for their children; screen time keeps the warring factions separate and quiet.

Thankfully, all family members can learn first to tolerate and accept and then to enjoy each other, regardless of age gap or differences in gender, temperament or interests. But it may not happen if you simply leave it to chance. You will probably need to do some things differently in order to achieve a different result.

Family Time is very useful for bringing siblings together and showing them that they can enjoy each other's company for longer and longer stretches of time. You may need to supervise it carefully at first to make sure it doesn't deteriorate into mayhem.

In my earlier books, *Calmer, Easier, Happier Parenting* and *Calmer, Easier, Happier Boys*, I explain strategies that parents can use to help siblings get on better.

Replacing screen time with Special Time

Special Time is one parent with one child, doing something you both enjoy. Special Time enables you to focus your attention on one child, which is enjoyable both for you and for your child. Without the undercurrent of sibling rivalry, you and your child can both relax. Special Time is an excellent remedy for electronic withdrawal pains.

Special Time is possibly a bit of a misnomer because what you and your child will be doing together is not a special treat. It's not about going somewhere special or getting a sweet treat or spending money. And it's definitely not happening in front of a screen. Special Time is you and your child alone together, enjoying each other's company. The activity you do together might be a game or a household task or a chat or going for a walk. What makes it Special Time is that your child has your undivided attention. You and your child should alternate who chooses the Special Time activity. When it's your turn to choose, make sure to choose activities that your child or teen would never choose. That way he is getting frequent exposure to activities that he otherwise might not realise he could enjoy.

If you're not yet in the habit of regularly spending Special Time with your child or teen, she may resist at first. Her reluctance may stem from an assumption that you're sure to find something she's done wrong to lecture her about. Or maybe she can't really believe that you enjoy her company enough to commit to spending time just with her on a daily basis. Persevere. Don't let her wriggle out of it. You will both soon come to treasure your Special Time together.

Preparing meals together as Special Time

Parents may be reluctant to make children earn their screen time if it's convenient to have the children occupied:

> 'They don't have much screen time, just while I'm making the tea. It keeps them from bickering or getting into something and making a mess.'

This is an example of using screen time as a sedative. Instead, each time you are preparing a meal, have one child with you in the kitchen, contributing. This accomplishes numerous goals:

- It is Special Time that you don't need to set aside any extra time for because you will be spending the time making the meal anyway.
- Over time your child will learn useful life skills of meal preparation.
- The children will learn to entertain themselves when it's not their turn in the kitchen.
- The children will be in separate rooms so they won't be able to bicker.
- Children are far more likely to eat and to enjoy food they were involved in preparing.
- You won't feel you need a machine to manage your child.
- Chatting while you are both engaged in a task is an ideal medium for transmitting our values. And relaxed, friendly conversations with parents are some of the best memories many adults have of their own childhoods.

There's something unique about the Special Time conversations that take place when a parent and child are involved in a task together. The parent is far less likely to ask the sorts of pointed questions that put children on the spot and make them feel they have to come up with the 'right' answer. When you're both focused on a task or activity, the conversation is more casual, more likely to digress. This helps children feel more relaxed, and they will often open up in a way that is much less likely to happen when you're looking them in the eye and trying to get an answer.

Parents sometimes worry when I suggest using meal preparation as Special Time:

'But then my other child feels left out and wants to help as well, and I can't have two children underfoot in my small kitchen.'

Just because the other child wants to join in does not mean you should let him. That would defeat the purpose of Special Time. Remember that children are experts in knowing what they want in the moment; we are the experts when it comes to knowing what children need in the long term. Children need to learn to play independently, not just when they happen to feel like it, but also when no sibling, playmate or parent is available or wants to play with them. Please read on for tips on how to teach and train children to play independently, even when they don't feel like it.

Teaching life skills during Special Time

Don't use your evenings after the children are in bed to get things done. Of course things need to get done, but many of these tasks can be done during the daylight hours if you are willing to involve your children. Cooking, cleaning, laundry, garden maintenance, DIY, errands, food shopping – these are all activities that you might think of as drudgery. But you can choose to see them as opportunities to enjoy being with your children. Of course, it will take longer to get things done if you involve your children, but you will be achieving four goals at the same time: getting your tasks done, spending enjoyable time with your children, teaching and training very useful life skills, and showing them that there's a lot more to life than screens. These goals are worth the bit of extra time you'll add to your tasks by including the children.

Not everything has to be fun

When we try to convince a child or teen to do something by promising, or even just suggesting, that it will be fun, this gives him the impression that everything has to be fun and that he shouldn't have to do it if he doesn't think it's going to be fun. We've seen how screen time blunts enjoyment of non-screen activities. So even if your child doesn't have a particularly tricky temperament, if he's used to spending a lot of time in front of a screen, after a while not much else will seem like fun. The antidote for this is Special Time.

Replacing screen time with independent play

For too many children, the words 'play' and 'game' describe something they do on a screen. The real-life pastimes and hobbies that have absorbed children for centuries, in fact for thousands of years, now seem old-fashioned and uncool. The more immersed children are in Screen World, the more it takes over the rest of their lives. There's not much time left in the day when children are thrown back on their own resources and have to make their own entertainment – even if it's just daydreaming. It's through unstructured time in the real world that children and teens learn to process their experiences and feelings, to make transitions, to solve the little problems that arise, to discover what they enjoy doing, to self-soothe when things don't go as they hoped or expected. Research indicates that physically touching and moving three-dimensional objects, the way children do in real play, improves sensory-motor skills and visual-motor skills. These skills are impor-tant for learning mathematics and science, as well as for real life of course.

Gwen Denar PhD, founder of the website 'Parenting Science', writes:

'Electronic entertainment may crowd out creative play. In one recent study, researchers analysed children's everyday schedules and noticed a link between screen time and the neglect of play. For every hour of TV watched each week, kids experienced a ten percent reduction in creative activities, like make-believe, arts and crafts and playing with non-electronic toys.'

And even when children are playing real-life games, too often the themes and characters are borrowed from their screen preoccupations.

Weekends and school holidays – that's when parents most dread the words, *'I'm bored'*. When children say they are bored, often it's another way of saying that no activity has been planned for them or no one is available, or willing, to play with them. When children say, *'There's nothing to do,'* it's never true. That complaint just means that at that moment none of their toys or books or hobbies appeals to them. When parents suggest possible activities, a child who is in a 'bored' mood will shoot down each suggestion with *'That's boring'*. Usually the only thing that appeals to a bored child is a screen. Have you ever known a child to reject the suggestion of a screen? Probably never.

Children are not likely to put much effort into thinking about what they could do for fun as long as there is a chance that they can get some screen time – by pestering, pleading, persuading, negotiating, bargaining, lying or by sneaking off to a screen that's not password-protected in another part of the house. This is one important reason why we need to have clear rules about screen time and to enforce them consistently. Otherwise children and teens can easily become too dependent on screens as a quick fix whenever they don't know what to do with themselves. So let's allow children to feel 'bored' so that they realise that they can find something interesting to do that's not screen-related.

Most children will play by themselves when they feel like it. But they also need to develop the confidence that they can entertain themselves when they don't feel like it, for example when they would rather be on a screen. A very useful strategy for establishing this habit is 'independent play.'

Every day, and twice a day at weekends and during the holidays, have a designated time when all of the children have to go to separate rooms for a specified length of time. Start with a short amount of time and gradually lengthen it. There may be some initial resistance, but soon they will become more comfortable with their own company, and they will find that they actually enjoy many non-screen activities. This will help them, over time, to become less fixated on screens.

When your child or teen gets into the habit of playing alone, without any screens, for a period of time every day, she will become more resilient and more self-reliant. She'll become more skilled at problem-solving and more confident. Here's another reason why your child needs to develop the habit of playing alone, even when she would rather not. It's an important step on the path towards being able to do schoolwork or homework by herself, even when she would rather not.

You can expect resistance at first, so be prepared to supervise the independent play to make sure it's really happening. Routines reduce resistance so as much as possible arrange for the independent play to happen at the same time every day. But if that's not convenient, plan when it will happen at least a day in advance so that you can let the children know. All children, but especially those with a more intense or inflexible temperament, will be more cooperative if we give them some time to get used to having to do what we ask of them.

Independent play for young children

This mother spoke for many when she raised this objection to teaching and training independent play:

> *'I do see the point of teaching my children to play alone. Then I could have Special Time with one or I could help one with revision or piano practice without having to rely on the TV or my phone to keep the other ones occupied. But my children are too young and too active and impulsive to be left alone. Help!'*

There are a number of possible solutions to this problem:

- Child-proof one room so that you know a young child cannot wreak havoc or hurt himself. I know this is easier said than done. You may need to put puzzles and games with lots of little pieces beyond reach. If your child is a climber, you may need to remove all the chairs.

- Make the room where your child will be playing alone close to whichever room you will be in. That way you can easily keep tabs on him.
- If child-proofing one room is totally impractical, often it's possible to section off a corner of one room with low fencing, like a baby gate. Or you can put tape on the floor to mark off a corner of one room and train him to stay within that area. Here's how: before you start preparing the dinner or doing anything that requires your concentration, set out in that area some especially appealing toys, and make sure those toys are not available at any other times so that they retain their novelty value. Get your child used to having to stay in this area by practising the independent play several times a day, starting with just a few minutes at a time and putting him back, gently but firmly, every time he steps an inch over the line. Descriptively Praise him after every few minutes that he stays in the right place.

You may object to all these strategies:

'But he would cry and cry if he had to stay in the room on his own or in a special corner of the kitchen.'

Yes, at first he might cry, especially if until now when he cried you usually picked him up. But within a few days he will get used to entertaining himself when you put him there if you remain calm (at least on the outside); if you keep acting as if you are confident that he's absolutely fine there by himself; if you Descriptively Praise him a lot for staying where you've told him to stay; if you remember to smile – and if you persevere.

But is all this teaching and training really worth it? Or are the sobs and screams a sign that you're being cruel? What I'm suggesting may seem like a huge, unnecessary palaver when you could easily switch on the television or a film or hand him your phone for twenty minutes while you get on with whatever you want to concentrate on. But this strategy of training independent play is really what countless generations of parents did, without even realising they were doing it, up until television became a fixture in most homes. It's what millions of parents the world over still do, in all the parts of the world where electronics are not yet a way of life.

> **How the habit of independent play can help with sibling rivalry**
> When siblings are squabbling or teasing each other, parents often separate them, or threaten to. I recommend not reacting in this way because it gives the siblings attention for the squabbling, and it sends the message that you think they can't learn to get on with each other. The time to separate children is long before there is a problem, and the way to do it is with the daily independent play. Siblings usually get on well after they have been apart for a while.

Remember how motivating Descriptive Praise (see Chapter 13) can be? If your child is upset about the independent play, Descriptively Praise him every few minutes:

'You're not calling down the hall for your brother.'

'You've found some books to look at.'

'You're staying in the right place.'

Reflective Listening (see Chapter 16) will also help him get over the upset of not being entertained:

'You're not used to playing all by yourself.'

'Maybe ten minutes is feeling like ten hours!'

'You probably wish we didn't have these new rules.'

And for maximum impact you can combine Descriptive Praise and Reflective Listening:

'Even though you wish you could be on your phone right now, I see you've found something to do until the timer goes ding.'

Playing-alone time helped wean Tom off screens
The girls have always been good at playing by themselves or playing together, but Tom was the odd one out. He used to tease the girls or ruin their games, or he'd be hanging around in the kitchen, whingeing that he was bored and that he wanted to go on the computer. It seemed like he really didn't know what to do with himself when no entertainment was laid on.

When we read in Noël's book about teaching children to play independently, we thought it was worth giving it a go for a month to see if it would help. So we made a time every day when all three had to play in separate rooms. It was easy for the girls, but Tom acted like we were the worst parents in the world. But we stayed firm. The Reflective Listening helped. So did the Descriptive Praise and the *think-throughs*.

Six months on, we're still doing it. The playing-alone time has made Tom much more self-reliant. He suddenly seemed more grown-up. And we can leave him to get on with his homework now because he's more confident. I think that's because he's had lots of experience during playing-alone time when he has to come up with his own solutions when he's got a problem. And he doesn't feel the need to keep bothering his sisters any more. He accepts the screen time rules, instead of always wanting more. So many benefits from this one strategy!

Father of Tom (aged 8),
Amanda (aged 5) and Lola (aged 4)

Replacing screen time with exercise

It's hard enough to get children, and especially teens, outside when the weather is good; many would rather stay indoors and immerse themselves in Screen World. Getting children to play outside when it's cold or wet can be even more of a struggle. Electronics become all the more appealing.

The current guidelines recommend that all children should have at least an hour of really intense physical activity every day. Many do not get anything close to an hour, and I have found that boys often need even more than an hour. This is especially true of those boys who are less mature or who have a more extreme temperament. It may require some creativity and ingenuity on your part to arrange the family's schedule so that there is enough time for your children to get rid of all their excess energy. But it's worth it!

Whenever possible make a point of taking the children straight from school to the park and letting them tear around and climb and play noisily for an hour or so. Although this puts the afternoon and evening routine back by an hour, you will end up saving time. Instead of trying to push and cajole an immovable object to do the things he doesn't feel like doing, you'll be dealing with someone who is much more willing, more relaxed, more cooperative.

If we want our children to be easier to live with, they need exercise <u>every day</u>, even when the weather isn't agreeable. If they have absorbed the message that there's something wrong with getting cold or wet, they may resist. The solution is to go outdoors with them and show them how much fun it can be:

- dancing, singing and shouting in the rain
- making an obstacle course out of what's lying around
- searching for bugs and worms
- racing
- inventing silly walks, etc.

Instead of trying to persuade, make a rule. If you have already put in place a rule that screen time is earned by first-time cooperation, all you will need to do (and it may not even be necessary) is to give the instruction about exercise and then say something like '*I hope you cooperate without any arguing. I want you to stay on track for earning your screen time.*'

If it's really impossible for your children and teens to spend time outdoors, you will need to arrange for indoor exercise. If your children or teens are not excited about the prospect of indoor exercise, don't try to sell it to them. Don't try to convince them that once they get started they'll enjoy it. That's usually true, but not always. A child who has an inflexible tempera- ment may not find that he enjoys it, but that is beside the point. Whether he enjoys it or not, he needs the exercise because it's good for his body, his brain, his mood – and because it reduces screen dependency, both in the short term and the long term.

What sorts of exercise can you and your children do indoors?

- rebounding on a mini-trampoline
- dancing
- star jumps
- marching in place with knees high
- stretches
- lifting weights (to save money these can be fashioned from household objects)
- push-ups
- yoga
- Wii Sports

Many parents have told me that once they realised it was their job to make sure that their children and teens burned off their excess energy every day, everything at home became much calmer, easier and happier. Cooperation and self-reli- ance improved. Screen dependency was vastly reduced. Sibling relationships, attitude towards authority, attention to detail with homework, sleep habits, willingness to eat what was put in front of them – all these aspects of family life improved because the children were less irritable and less easily frustrated when they got plenty of exercise on most days.

Replacing the use of screens when children have to wait

We hear a lot nowadays about resilience and 'grit'. Resilience is usually defined as the ability to withstand or recover quickly from difficult conditions. The definition of grit is often given as courage or resolve or determination. Parents, teachers and psychologists are concerned that modern children and teens are too ready to give up when the going gets tough, that they're unwilling to take healthy risks.

Technology plays a part in this worrying trend. In the past generation or two, we have come to see boredom as a problem that needs to be fixed. Think about the times when children have to wait – in a restaurant, in a queue, at the supermarket, at the dentist, on a long car journey. Before hand-held electronic devices, mobile phones and tablets, children were thrown back on their own resources. They had to occupy themselves. While waiting, a child might chat to the parent, or he could read or draw if he or the parent had thought ahead and brought a book or some paper and markers. Failing that, children looked around, noticing and wondering, or they stared into space, letting their imagination take them goodness knows where. Children learned that boredom doesn't kill you. Children learned, without realising they were learning it, that they had inner resources they could rely on.

Nowadays when you see a child who is waiting with a parent, he is likely to have a mobile phone or a tablet in his hand. It is so rare to see a waiting child reading a book or having a lively conversation with a parent that it has started to look unfamiliar and odd. Why isn't the waiting child chatting with a parent? Because often the parent is flicking through his or her mobile, unavailable for interacting with.

Here's how parents explain why they allow, or even encourage, screens during waiting times:

'Let's face it, long car journeys are a nightmare for children. It's not fair to expect them to entertain themselves for hours.'

'In a restaurant it keeps him from playing with the cutlery or pouring the salt on the table, or trying to get down and run around, which would disturb the other people.'

'He gets so restless standing in line. If I don't give him my phone to play with, he'll drive me mad with his whingeing or endless questions or silly jokes.'

Two related assumptions have become increasingly widespread. One is that waiting is too hard on children, too frustrating and too boring, so parents should fix this problem by providing some entertaining distractions. And a fool-proof way of doing this is with electronics. The other assumption is that parents are at the mercy of a child who is whingeing, bickering, interrupting or wandering off. If parents don't know how to improve a child's behaviour, they'll feel the need to use distraction to manage the situation. And what's guaranteed to distract successfully? Electronics, of course. This way of coping with waiting has become the norm.

When I suggest alternatives to handing a complaining child an electronic device, parents may ask, *'What's so bad about distracting a bored or restless child with a bit of electronic entertainment?'* There is nothing 'bad' about using electronics as a distraction. But it does lead to several undesirable outcomes:

- This habit reinforces our belief that children can't learn to cope with mild discomfort.
- And soon children themselves start to believe that they can't tolerate the frustration of having to wait.
- Children may come to believe that they should not have to experience anything that is less than pleasant.
- Following on from the above beliefs, children may assume that it's the parents' job to rescue them from frustration and boredom by laying on some riveting entertainment.

It's important for children to develop resilience and grit and self-reliance. We can help our children develop these qualities by allowing them to experience the natural, normal, inevitable feelings of frustration, annoyance, restlessness and boredom. Let's not jump in and rescue them from their uncomfortable feelings. We want to show, by our words, by our tone of voice, by our body language and by our actions, that there is nothing wrong. A long wait is not a problem that needs to be fixed. Instead of unintentionally weakening our children, we can use the Calmer, Easier, Happier Parenting strategies to reinforce the useful habits of resilience, self-reliance and grit:

- First make a new rule, or reactivate an old rule that you haven't been following through on consistently. This might be:

  'From now on when we're waiting for Jack's music lesson to finish, we can play talking games, or we can chat, but you won't be on my phone, and neither will I.'

  'The new rule is that when we're in the car going to Granny's, for the first hour we'll play games or sing or chat,

*or we can just be silent. And what do think your reward for
an hour of no arguing or whingeing will be?*

You might require a shorter or longer period of time for cooperative, polite behaviour before he earns the reward, depending on your child's age, temperament and how long you know
he can behave well for.

- Then Prepare for Success (see Chapter 15) by doing
  think-throughs at neutral times:

  *'If you're in a queue and you're feeling frustrated or restless,
  what could you do to take your mind off it?'*

  *'Tomorrow when we're sitting in the waiting room at
  the dentist's office, what could we do to pass the time?'*

  *'In the airport and on the plane, what could you do for fun
  since you won't have any electronics?'*

- During the waiting, remember to Descriptively Praise
  (see Chapter 13):

  'You're not complaining.'

  *'You could see I was talking to the waitress, and you didn't
  interrupt.'*

  'You're playing by yourself.'

- We can also Reflectively Listen (see Chapter 16) when
  they complain or cry about the new rule:

'It sounds like you're furious. Probably you're wishing
Mummy and Daddy hadn't made a new rule about no
electronics in the car.'

Let's look at the types of situations in which you and your children will have to wait and explore alternatives to using screens to prevent misbehaviour.

Standing and waiting

Children love interacting with their parents, chatting or playing, and you probably enjoy it too – once you set aside your phone and your preoccupations, once you commit to paying attention to the childish conversation for five or ten minutes. Think of it as Special Time. Children learn so much about how the world works through conversations with an interested adult. And parents learn so much about their children through the give-and-take of casual conversation. We learn far more than when we ask questions like, *'What did you do in school today?'*, which are often met with a grunt or a shrug or *'I dunno'.*

Take turns pointing out things of interest in your surroundings. This leads children to notice and think about aspects of their environment that they may have been oblivious to.

Below are some games you can play

I Spy

This versatile game can be adapted for toddlers all the way through to teens by making the clues easier or more challenging. For example, if you 'spied' a picture of an elephant, you might say (in ascending order of challenge):

'I spy a picture of . . .
- an animal that has a trunk
- a big animal
- an animal, and it begins with the sounds "eleph . . ."
- an animal that might be called Babar
- an animal, and its name starts with the short "e" sound
- an animal, and there are three syllables in its name
- an animal with eight letters in its name
- an animal whose native habitat is Africa and India
- an animal that can give itself a shower
- an animal that is sometimes hunted for its ivory
- an animal that can carry people on its back'
- an animal that is sometimes used as a beast of burden

Alphabet words

Together you agree on a category (foods, jobs, books, given names, famous people, adjectives, etc). Then starting with 'A' and continuing through the alphabet, you each take turns thinking of a word in that category that starts with the next letter of the alphabet. If your child is stuck, you can give clues, but don't tell him the answer, and don't let him skip his turn or give up altogether.

A huge amount of incidental learning takes place during this game; you can clear up misconceptions and fill in gaps in your child's general knowledge. A more challenging version of this game is to have each person start their next turn by repeating all the alphabet words said so far, starting from A each time.

I wonder

Taking turns, you and your child look around you until you find something that you realise you don't know very much about. Then together you talk about that topic.

Here are some 'wonderings' I've collected from parents who have introduced this game to their children:

'I wonder who invented the first postage stamp.'
'I wonder if banks ever run out of money.'
'I wonder how they make concrete.'

Together make up a story
Alternating turns, you each add the next sentence to the story.

Practise five minutes (no more) of something your child needs to memorise for school
Number bonds, multiplication facts, spellings, French verbs, physics formulae. If you keep it very short and remember to smile and Descriptively Praise (see Chapter 13), your child will probably enjoy it.

Sitting and waiting
All of the above activities, plus:

- Play one of the ten paper-and-pencil thinking games from *Calmer, Easier, Happier Homework* (pages 154–161).
- Play the 'Go Game' from *Calmer, Easier, Happier Boys* (pages 229–232). This is another extremely versatile game that can be tweaked for any age.
- Reading (separately or together).
- Drawing.
- In the car: singing.
- In a waiting room you can tell the person on the desk that you and your children will be waiting outside and will be back in about ten minutes, for example. Outside, the children can let off steam by playing more active

games. If you're with one child, you can turn this into Special Time.

If siblings are liable to hassle each other, sit them on either side of you, rather than next to each other. If you're all sitting at a table, have them sit diagonally across from each other so they are as far apart as possible.

CONCLUSION

Having read this far, I imagine that you've already started experimenting with some of the strategies that I recommend in this book, and probably you've seen some progress. But I'm sure you've also experienced that some days are better than others — life is like that! In case you're feeling discouraged because parenting isn't plain sailing, I'll repeat what I've said periodically throughout the book: persevere. It will get easier and easier — if you don't give up.

To remind you of what you can achieve, here are the experiences of four families who committed to getting back in charge of the screens in their homes:

'When Ben and Lucy were in primary school, I couldn't really understand what the other mums were talking about when they were complaining about how technology was taking over their family. But by the time the twins were in secondary school, I understood because I was living with it! Checking their phone messages and tweets and updating their status every day seemed much more interesting than talking to me or their dad or doing their homework. Every once in a while we tried making rules, but I realise now why it didn't work. We were reacting in anger, and not thinking things through, so there were always too many loopholes.

This all changed when we learned about the three stages of being in charge. We followed Noël's plan to the letter. For the first week or two we were holding our breath, waiting for *the explosion. But it went better than we thought it would. Of course they didn't like the new rules, but they didn't actually refuse because we did it in stages. First we did lots of Descriptive Praise and Special Time and independent play, then the limits plan, then a few weeks later we told them they had to earn their screen time. The Special Time and Family Time really helped. It gave them something fun to look forward to that wasn't just a screen. Of course they still love their screen time, but now they have lots of other interests and hobbies as well.'*

Mother of twins Lucy and Ben (aged 13)

'Up until about two years ago, my son was addicted to computer games. It's what he lived for. It seemed like he hadn't picked up a book in years unless he had to for school, and his homework was scruffy and the bare minimum. Anything I asked him to do caused an argument. I kept putting off doing anything about it because it all seemed too complicated, and I couldn't really believe anything would work. I'm a single parent, and when Joe goes to his dad's there are no rules, so I felt overwhelmed.

But finally I'd had enough because we were having so many rows. I got up my courage and did what Noël suggests – new rules and rewards, Descriptive Praise and Reflective Listening and all the other strategies. The first three weeks were the worst. Lots of arguing and shouting. From him, not from me. I kept re-reading Noël's books to stay calm and determined. And it worked!

Joe is sixteen now, and it's hard to remember how bad things were. Now he's doing really well at school, and he's proud of his good marks. He's helpful. He follows the screen rules. He's a pleasure!'

Mother of Joe (aged 16)

'My husband and I used to argue a lot about how to handle screen time. He was fed up with coming home after a long day and wanting to spend time with the kids, but they would barely look up from their computers. I hate to admit it but I was the softie. To be honest, I used to let them get away with so much screen time because it was easier. I didn't have to listen to the whingeing and fighting.

It got so bad that we even talked about divorce a few times. That was a wake-up call for us both. We decided we had better become a United Front, as Noël calls it. So we did. We started with the Descriptive Praise and Reflective Listening and Special Time before we even made any new rules because we thought that might make the adjustment easier, and it definitely did help. When we made the new rules, they accepted them pretty well. The children became so much nicer. Now we have lots of fun as a family without screens, and my husband and I never talk about divorce now – thank goodness!'

Mother of Sarah (aged 15) and Craig (aged 12)

'My wife and I realised we were setting our children a terrible example. The TV was on in the background a lot, when no one was really watching. And my wife and I would check our messages and emails a lot, even when we didn't really need to. We had a couple of big TV screens, including one in our bedroom.

When we realised this we were quite ashamed of ourselves so we decided we should clean up our own act before we made any new rules for the children. So we got rid of the TV in our bedroom. We sold it, and with the money we got for it we took the children to a theme park. They loved that and asked if we could sell another TV to get another treat – so we did! But it wasn't all grand gestures. We also made sure the *children saw us reading every day, a proper book, not just a magazine, even if it was only for five minutes. Soon they would come and cuddle up next to us with their own books.*

My wife bought a second-hand encyclopedia from the charity shop, and we started looking things up, not just Googling. We started dropping by the library every Saturday on the way to the supermarket. And instead of family film night on Fridays, we decided to have games night – good old-fashioned games like Boggle and cards and draughts.

What amazed us is that the children started spending less time on their screens even before we introduced the new rules. It really shows how much they copy us. Now that we realise that, we make sure to set them a good example about a lot of other things, to get them into good habits.'

Father of Louise (aged 15),
Philip (aged 10) and Graham (aged 9)

You can create similar results in your home. So get started and keep going. Soon you'll have a calmer, easier, happier family.

CALMER, EASIER, HAPPIER PARENTING RESOURCES

Noël Janis-Norton is the director of the Calmer, Easier, Happier Parenting Centre, a not-for-profit consultancy and training organisation that works worldwide with families and also with a range of professionals who work with families, including teachers and social workers.

The team of certified parenting practitioners includes parent coaches, family coaches and group facilitators. They work with families whose children and teenagers are experiencing problems with learning, confidence, motivation and behaviour, ranging from mild to severe.

The Centre offers the following services:
Introductory talks for parents (at the Centre, in schools and in the workplace)
Parenting skills courses
Seminars and webinars
Private consultations (at the Centre, by telephone or in the home)
School visits to observe a child and guide teachers
Mediation between parents
Teacher-training

In addition, the Centre offers books and audio CDs on many aspects of parenting and teaching.

CDs about the five core strategies of Calmer Easier, Happier Parenting:
Descriptive Praise
Preparing for Success
Reflective Listening
Never Ask Twice
Rewards and Consequences

Topic CD sets:
Siblings with Less Rivalry (3 discs)
Calmer, Easier, Happier Mealtimes (2 discs)
Calmer, Easier, Happier Music Practice (2 discs)
Bringing Out the Best in Children and Teens with Special Needs (5 discs)

Books for parents:
Calmer, Easier, Happier Parenting by Noël Janis-Norton
Calmer, Easier, Happier Homework by Noël Janis-Norton
Calmer, Easier, Happier Boys by Noël Janis-Norton
How to Calm a Challenging Child by Miriam Chachamu
How to Be a Better Parent by Cassandra Jardine
Positive Not Pushy by Cassandra Jardine
Girls, Uninterrupted by Tanith Carey

Books for teachers:
These books are filled with proven techniques that teachers can use to rapidly improve the learning, behaviour, motivation and confidence of their pupils.

In Step with Your Class by Noël Janis-Norton
Learning to Listen, Listening to Learn by Noël Janis-Norton

For more information about the Calmer, Easier, Happier Parenting and Teaching resources, please visit the following websites:

www.calmerparenting.co.uk (UK)
www.calmerparenting.com (North America)
www.calmerparenting.fr (France)

APPENDIX B:
OTHER RESOURCES

There are many useful websites that offer excellent advice to parents who are committed to getting back in charge of the technology in their home.

I've listed below some of the websites that my clients have found especially helpful, but don't be limited by these.

Revision websites:
BBC.co.uk/education
Examsolutions.net
Getrevising.co.uk
Khanacademy.org
S-cool.co.uk

Websites with lists of non-violent and non-sexist online educational games for children and teens:
Aleteia.org
Commonsensemedia.org
Netmums.com
Newkidscenter.com
Parenting.com
Stayathomemoms.about.com
Todaysparent.com

Here is a selection of websites that explain how to use various types of parental controls. The instructions are not always easy to understand, but the large measure of peace of mind they can bring makes persevering well worth the effort:

About.com/parenting

Childnet.com

Howtogeek.com

Internetmatters.org

Internet-filters.net (B safe online)

Internetsafety.com (Safe Eyes)

Netgear.com

Netnanny.com

Onguardonline.gov

Ofcom.org.uk

Parentalcontrolbar.com

Saferinternet.org

Staysafeonline.org

Techradar.com

Thinkuknow.co.uk

Wikipedia.org

In addition, every brand of electronic device explains online exactly how to activate the parental controls that are built into that device.

Probably none of the parental controls are completely fool-proof. A very tech-savvy young person would eventually be able to circumvent many of them, but in most cases he or she will only be motivated to defy you to that extent if the parent-child relationship has deteriorated significantly. In this book I have explained how getting back in charge of screen time in your home can help you to re-establish calmer, easier, happier family relationships.

INDEX

Other books by Noël Janis-Norton are available in paperback, ebook and audiobook